ENVIRONMENTAL DISASTERS

The Chernobyl Nuclear Disaster

W. Scott Ingram

☑®
Facts On File, Inc.

The Chernobyl Nuclear Disaster

Facts On File, Inc.
132 West 31st Street
New York NY 10001

Library of Congress Cataloging-in-Publication Data
Ingram, Scott.
  The Chernobyl nuclear disaster / W. Scott Ingram.
      p. cm. — (Environmental disasters)
  Includes bibliographical references and index.
  ISBN 0-8160-5755-9 (hc: acid-free paper)
    1. Chernobyl Nuclear Accident, Chernobyl, Ukraine, 1986—Juvenile
  literature. 2. Disasters—Environmental aspects—Juvenile literature.
  3. Nuclear power plants—Ukraine—Chernobyl—Accidents—Juvenile
  literature. I. Title. II. Environmental disasters (Facts On File)
TK1362.U281575 2005
363.17'99'094776—dc22   2004063409

Facts On File books are available at special discounts when purchased in bulk quantities for businesses, associations, institutions, or sales promotions. Please call our Special Sales Department in New York at (212) 967-8800 or (800) 322-8755.

You can find Facts On File on the World Wide Web at http://www.factsonfile.com

A Creative Media Applications, Inc. Production
Writer: W. Scott Ingram
Design and Production: Alan Barnett, Inc.
Editor: Matt Levine
Copy Editor: Laurie Lieb
Proofreaders: Laurie Lieb and Tania Bissell
Indexer: Nara Wood
Associated Press Photo Researcher: Yvette Reyes
Consultant: Thomas A. Birkland, Nelson A. Rockefeller College of Public Affairs
    and Policy, University at Albany, State University of New York
Diagrams by Rolin Graphics

Printed in the United States of America

VB PKG   10 9 8 7 6 5 4 3 2 1

This book is printed on acid-free paper.

Contents

Preface

This book is about the nuclear accident at the Chernobyl nuclear power plant in the former Soviet Union. On April 26, 1986, a massive explosion blew the roof off the plant's Reactor Four and sent radioactive dust into the air. The map on the next page shows the parts of Europe that were affected by radiation from the disaster.

Almost everyone is curious about such catastrophic events. An interest in these disasters, as shown by the decision to read this book, is the first step on a fascinating path toward learning how disasters occur, why they are feared, and what can be done to prevent them from hurting people, as well as their homes and businesses.

The word *disaster* comes from the Latin for "bad star." Thousands of years ago, people believed that certain alignments of the stars influenced events on Earth, including natural disasters. Today, natural disasters are sometimes called "acts of God" because no human made them happen. Scientists now know that earthquakes, hurricanes, and volcanic eruptions occur because of natural processes that the scientists can explain much better than they could even a few years ago.

An event is usually called a disaster only if it hurts people. For example, an earthquake occurred along Alaska's Denali fault in 2002. Although this earthquake had a magnitude of 7.9, it killed no one and did little serious damage. But a "smaller" earthquake—with a magnitude below 7.0—in Kobe, Japan, in 1995 did billions of dollars in damage and killed about 5,100 people. This quake was considered a disaster.

A disaster may also damage animals and the environment. The *Exxon Valdez* oil spill in Alaska is considered a disaster because it injured and killed hundreds of birds, otters, deer, and other animals. The spill also killed thousands of fish—which

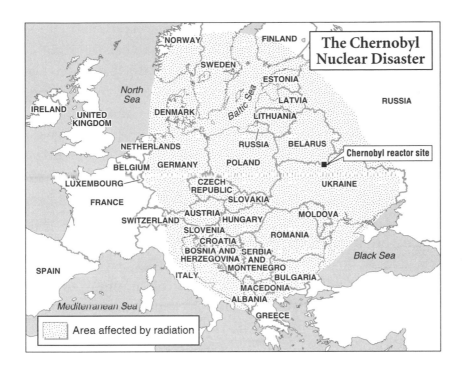

Area affected by radiation

many Alaskan fishers rely on to earn their livelihoods—and polluted the places where the fish spawn.

Disasters are also more likely to happen when people make decisions that leave them *vulnerable* to catastrophe. For example, a beachside community is more vulnerable to a hurricane than a community that is inland from the ocean. When people choose where to live, they are also choosing what sort of natural disasters they may experience in the future; they are choosing the sort of risks they are willing to take. People who live on beaches in Florida know that hurricanes may damage or destroy their houses; people who live in certain areas of California know that earthquakes may strike at any time.

The things that people do to make themselves safer from less dangerous natural events, like heavy rains, sometimes actually make the people more vulnerable to bigger disasters. For example, when a dam is built on a river to protect people downstream from floods, the dam may prevent small floods that would otherwise happen once every 25 years. But when a really big storm occurs—the kind that comes once every 100 years—the dam may not be able to hold back the water. Then a surge of water that is even bigger than it would have been without the dam will come rushing down the river and completely destroy all the buildings in the area.

At first, it may seem easy to blame human disasters, like the *Exxon Valdez* spill, on one or a few people. Some observers blame the spill on the captain, who was responsible for the ship. But perhaps the spill was another crewmember's fault. Maybe the blame should fall on Exxon, because that corporation owned the ship. Or maybe all Americans are to blame, because the United States uses a lot of oil for heating houses and driving cars. Finding the "right people" to blame can be difficult. Is it anyone's fault that people suffer from natural disasters? Natural disasters at first appear to be merely unfortunate "acts of God."

This book and the other books in this series will demonstrate that mistakes people made before a disaster often made the disaster worse than it should have been. But they will also show how many people work to lessen the damage caused by disasters. Firefighters, sailors, and police officers, for example, work very hard right after disasters to rescue people, limit additional damage, and help people get back to their normal lives. Behind the scenes are engineers, architects, legislators, scientists, and other citizens working to design new buildings, make new rules about how and where to build buildings, and enforce those rules so that fewer people will have to risk their lives due to disasters.

The books in this series will show what can be done to reduce the chances that people and communities will suffer from natural and human disasters. Everyone has a role to play in making communities safer. The books in this series can show readers how to become part of a growing movement of citizens and experts that can help everyone make good decisions about disasters.

Please note: All metric conversions in this book are approximate.

Introduction

The progress of technology has brought the world a type of environmental disaster that was never seen before the mid-20th century: the *nuclear* accident. Since nuclear power was first used to generate electricity in the early 1950s, there have been relatively few such accidents. But because the health and environmental damage caused by the *radioactivity* of nuclear materials may last for centuries, it is difficult to calculate the overall effect of nuclear accidents.

Although assessing overall damage is difficult, scientists generally agree that the worst nuclear power disaster in history took place at the Chernobyl power station in the former Soviet Union (now the country of Ukraine) in April 1986. In that instance, a faulty design caused a *nuclear reactor* to overheat and explode. In the aftermath of the explosion, inadequate safety preparations and poor communication worsened the disaster.

The death toll as a result of the blast and radiation exposure was originally listed at 31 people. Soviet authorities initially said the radioactive *fallout* from the blast affected an area that extended no farther than an 18.6-mile (30-km) radius from the power plant. This area included the city of Pripyat, home to thousands of Chernobyl workers and their families, which was evacuated.

At first glance, the toll of the Chernobyl accident might seem insignificant compared to the thousands of people killed in typhoons, for example, or the enormous areas destroyed by forest fires. Yet in certain ways, the Chernobyl explosion was one of the most serious environmental disasters of the 20th century. The scope of the disaster was magnified by the initial efforts of the Soviet government to prevent news of the explosion and fallout from reaching Soviet citizens and the outside world. Even in Pripyat, a city just a few miles from the explosion, news of the event

This photograph, taken in 1998, shows the Chernobyl nuclear power plant in Ukraine. (Photo courtesy of Associated Press)

was downplayed. The order to evacuate the city was not given until nearly 40 hours after the explosion. By that time, many of the residents had suffered varying degrees of radioactive poisoning.

This failure to alert the residents of Pripyat and the country at large about the Chernobyl accident may have made the disaster even worse. Authorities took very few safety precautions to guard the public's health. Many of the firefighters who responded to the emergency lacked masks and other safety protection against radioactivity. The workers who came to the power plant to clean up the damage were also uninformed about the hazards they faced.

Because radioactivity can poison human bodies and pollute a large area for decades, it is almost impossible to calculate the overall toll of the Chernobyl disaster. Medical researchers today attribute a rise in cancer among people of the region to the fallout from the blast. The water and soil of thousands of square miles of modern Ukraine, Belarus, and Russia—countries once under control of the Soviet Union—will remain polluted for centuries.

In addition to the damage to health and the environment, the fact that the Soviet government hid the news of the event caused psychological damage to hundreds of thousands of people in the three countries most affected. The so-called Chernobyl Syndrome was an irrational psychological fear that resulted from the secrecy and deception of the Soviet leaders. Thus, the damage from Chernobyl has extended far beyond the 31 deaths and the poisoned environment. Chernobyl is a symbol of the damage that can result not from nature gone wild, but from human error and dishonesty.

The Chernobyl Nuclear Disaster explains the circumstances that led to the nuclear accident at Chernobyl. The book also tells the critically important story of the cover-up of the disaster that in many ways worsened the long-term effects on both people and the environment. The book concludes with a time line, a chronology of other nuclear plant accidents around the world, a glossary, and a list of sources (books and web sites) for further information.

Please note: Glossary words are in italics the first time that they appear in the text. Other words defined in the text may also be in italics.

CHAPTER 1

The Hidden Disaster

In 1986 the Union of Soviet Socialist Republics (USSR), also known as the Soviet Union, was the largest nation in the world in land area, extending from the Baltic Sea in the west to the Pacific Ocean in the east and covering over 8.6 million square miles (22.3 million km^2). The Soviet Union comprised 15 nations that today are independent, but at that time were controlled by a *Communist* government headquartered in Moscow, Russia. (The names of these nations can be found in the "Former Soviet Union" sidebar on page 2.)

   Among the nations in the Soviet Union was Ukraine, a huge agricultural region southwest of Moscow. Like the Plains states of the United States, Ukraine was considered the breadbasket of the

Ukraine, before the 1986 nuclear accident at Chernobyl, was a large agricultural region that supplied much of the food and grain for the Soviet Union. The catastrophe at Chernobyl destroyed crops and farmland for at least 100 miles (161 km) around for an unknown number of years. (Photo courtesy of Dean Conger/CORBIS)

Soviet Union. More than 40 percent of Ukraine's population worked on farms that supplied grain and other food crops to the entire Soviet Union.

The capital of Ukraine is Kiev, a city of more than 2 million people about 600 miles (965 km) southwest of Moscow. About 65 miles (105 km) north of Kiev, a dam across the mighty Dnieper River has created the huge Kiev Reservoir that supplies water to the millions of residents of the city. On the northern shore of the reservoir stood the ancient village of Chernobyl. Along the river about 15 miles (24 km) north of Chernobyl was the modern Soviet city of Pripyat. This city, with a population of 45,000, was situated on the border of Belarus, a small country wedged between Ukraine, Russia, and Poland.

In 1986, in a flat, 8.5-square-mile (22-km²) area between Chernobyl and the city of Pripyat, stood the V.I. Lenin Power Station. Named for the first leader of the Soviet Union, the station was commonly called the Chernobyl nuclear plant. The plant housed four enormous nuclear reactors and generated electricity for millions of people in Kiev, Pripyat, and much of the western Soviet Union.

The Former Soviet Union

The Soviet Union ceased to exist in 1991. Prior to that time, the 15 nations that made up the Soviet Union were Armenia, Azerbaijan, Belarus, Estonia, Georgia, Kazakhstan, Kyrgyzstan, Latvia, Lithuania, Moldavia, Russia, Tajikistan, Turkmenistan, Ukraine, and Uzbekistan. Of those nations, Russia was the largest in area and population. Ukraine was the second-largest in area and population.

Today, the entire Chernobyl plant is shut down, and the building that housed Reactor Four is buried under tons of sand and concrete. (More about this concrete "sarcophagus" can be found in Chapter 6.) The village is deserted, and the once-thriving city of Pripyat is a ghost town. In fact, the land around the plant for more than 30 miles (48 km) in every direction is uninhabited. Farmland sits unused, and nothing that grows there is safe for human consumption. Water in the region is not safe to drink. Scientists believe that the land and water will remain unsafe for centuries.

The empty, radiation-polluted land is the result of a chain of events that occurred over several days in late April 1986 at the Chernobyl power plant. The mishap was years in the making, and much of the blame for it has now been placed on Soviet scientists and government leaders, who not only ignored flaws in their nuclear power plants, but also refused to admit that a disaster had even occurred until days after it had taken place.

The Demand for Electricity

The Chernobyl plant originally opened in 1977. The plant had been constructed over a six-year period at a time when the Soviet Union, like all modern nations, faced enormous demands for electrical power to bring light, heat, and other necessities to millions of people. The main obstacle faced by nations in generating electricity at power plants was obtaining fuel to operate the plants. For much of the 20th century, as the use of electricity grew, coal, oil, or natural gas was used to fuel power plants.

By the end of World War II in 1945, a new source of energy had emerged—nuclear power. The destructive force of nuclear energy was demonstrated in 1945, when the United States, while at war with Japan, dropped atomic bombs on the Japanese cities of Hiroshima and Nagasaki, killing more than 200,000 people. Not only were the cities leveled, but also radioactive dust produced by the blasts—called fallout—caused enormous health and environmental damage.

By the late 1950s, scientists had learned to control nuclear power, and the new energy source was being used for purposes other than weapons. Naval vessels—aircraft carriers and submarines—were powered by nuclear energy, rather than gasoline. A method of generating electricity from nuclear fuel had led to the construction of nuclear power plants. Because the method of generating power was relatively untested, there was some concern in the scientific community that nuclear plant accidents might release radiation into the atmosphere. This led the United Nations (UN) to form the International Atomic Energy Agency (IAEA) in 1957. The IAEA established safe operating procedures and developed a system for reporting any safety violations. In general, however, nuclear power was considered cleaner and cheaper than energy generated from oil or coal.

By the 1980s, the Soviet Union was among the world's leading nations in the use of nuclear power, along with Great Britain, France, and the United States. More than 10 percent of all nuclear energy in the world was generated by 43 Soviet-made nuclear reactors. Four of the reactors were housed in the huge power station 2.1 miles (3.3 km) from the town of Pripyat.

Nuclear Power

The Chernobyl plant worked on the same principle as all power plants. The simplest way to understand the generation of electricity is to picture a water-filled teakettle on a stove with a pinwheel in front of the kettle's spout. Heat from the stove boils the kettle's water, creating steam. The steam inside the kettle eventually forces its way out of the spout, and the pressurized steam spins the blades on the pinwheel.

A power plant is basically an enormous stove powered by a fuel that generates heat, which, in turn, boils water. The steam from the water turns the blades of enormous engines called *turbines*. These turbines are like pinwheels. The turning motion creates electricity that can be either stored or carried to surrounding regions over power lines.

In a nuclear power plant, the "stove" is known as a nuclear reactor, and its heat is produced by the *element* uranium-235. The number 235 is affixed to the element because the *nucleus* of a single *atom* of *uranium* consists of 235 particles—92 *protons* and 143 *neutrons;* 92 is called its *atomic number*. By comparison, an atom of water has just three particles in its nucleus.

The Dangers of Nuclear Radiation

The danger from nuclear energy results from a by-product of the *fission* process. In addition to heat, some energy is released as radioactivity, which is highly poisonous. Exposure to large doses of radioactivity can interfere with cell development. Such exposure can lead to cell death or a change of cell structure called *mutation*—the origin of cancer—in plants, animals, and humans.

Radioactive rays to which one may be exposed are divided into three categories. The weakest are *alpha rays*—these turn skin red and cause swelling. They do not pass through the skin into the body, although breathing them can damage the cardiovascular system and lead to heart problems years later.

Beta rays can invade the internal organs through the skin. These rays cause cell mutation and damage. Exposure to beta rays during pregnancy is known to cause miscarriages, as well as birth defects.

Gamma rays are the most dangerous radioactive emissions. They enter the body through the skin and affect bone marrow, the intestinal system, and the thyroid gland. Cell mutations from gamma rays are known to cause various forms of cancer.

Uranium is one of the largest of all elements on what is known as the *periodic table*. Atoms at this end of this table are so large that they are almost too big to stay together permanently—therefore, scientists say that such atoms are *unstable*.

In an unstable element such as uranium-235, it is possible to speed up the breaking apart of its atoms by a process known as *induced fission*. Induced fission uses a "bombarding particle," a *neutron*, to split a target atom. The bombarding particle splits the target atom into two separate and nearly equal parts, releasing energy. These parts are known as *fission products*, and they contain most of the protons and neutrons of the original atom. Two or three spare neutrons are emitted, and some of the energy that was holding the atom together is given off as heat. (Another by-product of the fission reaction is described above in the "Dangers of Nuclear

Radiation" sidebar.) Once this action begins, it occurs over and over in other particles in what is known as a *chain reaction*.

To understand a chain reaction, scientists tell people to imagine a huge table completely covered with mousetraps. Each trap is set with a ping-pong ball on it. Imagine what would happen if an extra ping-pong ball were tossed onto the table. The bouncing action of the extra ball would spring a trap that would send its ball onto another trap, setting that trap off, and so on. The extra ping-pong ball is the bombarding neutron, and the mousetraps are uranium-235 atoms.

Most of the energy in a chain reaction is released in the form of intense heat. In fact, the energy given off by a uranium-235 chain reaction is so powerful that 1 pound (0.45 kg) of the element—an amount about the size of a baseball—can produce as much energy as 1 million gallons (3.8 million l) of gasoline.

The Challenges of Nuclear Power

In the 1950s, as the possibility of using nuclear power for peaceful purposes was realized, scientists faced two challenges. One challenge was to better aim the neutron "ping-pong balls" so that they were more likely to hit the uranium-235 atoms, the "mousetraps."

The other challenge was to slow the path of neutrons so that the "mousetraps" snapped in a controlled way. In their research, nuclear engineers discovered that neutrons travel more slowly if they have to force their way through certain atoms such as hydrogen or carbon before reaching the uranium-235 atoms. Thus, a key step in the development of nuclear reactors during the 1950s was the creation of reactor cores surrounding the uranium-235. The cores were also known as *moderators*, because they moderated—regulated—the number of neutrons that created the reaction. Using the stove comparison, the *core* became like the stove's burner.

In many nuclear reactors, including those in the United States, water is used as a moderator. In the Soviet-style nuclear

reactors, however, a form of carbon called graphite was used. Surrounding the uranium-235 with either of these materials slows the neutrons, helping them to hit their targets and making a controlled reaction possible.

Even with a moderator, a chain reaction could potentially send extra neutrons traveling randomly through the nuclear fuel, creating the explosive conditions of an atomic blast. In the course of research, scientists discovered that certain naturally occurring materials absorb neutrons without becoming unstable. The most common such material is an element called *boron,* which does not split when hit by random neutrons. This material was put into what were known as *control rods.* These devices slid between the fuel containers in the reactor core, absorbing extra neutrons like sponges. In effect, the control rods acted like the stove dial that controls the burner's heat. They absorbed neutrons that might otherwise create an uncontrolled chain reaction such as the one created when an atomic bomb is exploded.

By the early 1960s, nuclear scientists in several countries had developed methods for achieving a *controlled chain reaction.* To

The Soviet Union relied heavily on nuclear energy because other sources, like this dam and hydroelectric power plant, did not provide enough power for the country. (Photo courtesy of Dean Conger/CORBIS)

do this, they created a moderating core of water or graphite that held bundles of *fuel rods* containing uranium-235. Neutron-absorbing boron control rods were placed at points in the core to control the chain reaction.

In a nuclear reactor, a chain reaction is started by gradually withdrawing the boron control rods from the core, thus reducing the number of neutrons that are absorbed. Once the chain reaction is initiated, technicians carefully monitor and control the core temperature. When the temperature goes down, the control rods are slowly removed, meaning that fewer neutrons are absorbed. More unabsorbed neutrons mean more fission, which, in turn, means more energy and heat. When the temperature in the core rises past a certain level, the rods are slowly inserted back into the core to bring the temperature back down. To maintain a controlled nuclear chain reaction, the control rods are manipulated in such a way that each act of fission results in just one extra neutron "ping-pong ball" hitting one "mousetrap" atom, while the other neutrons are absorbed by control rods.

Nuclear Power Plants

Once researchers had developed methods to produce controlled chain reactions, nuclear power plants were built in many nations, such as the United States, Canada, Great Britain, Japan, and France, during the 1960s and 1970s. In those years, the main thrust of the anti-nuclear movement was concerned with the safe disposal of nuclear waste. Such waste remains radioactive for thousands of years. In the United States, for example, the anti-nuclear movement led to events such as the "No Nukes" concert held in Madison Square Garden in New York City in 1979. The concert featured popular artists such as Jackson Browne, James Taylor, and Bonnie Raitt, who performed for thousands of activists.

To fuel the reactors that ran the nuclear plants, uranium-235 was shaped into 1-inch (2.5-cm) pieces—about the diameter of a dime—called *pellets*. The pellets were inserted into long tubes called fuel rods or *assemblies* that were bundled together in the core. The core was usually submerged in water that produced steam for the turbines and served as a cooling system.

In a nuclear reactor, the core's uranium fuel bundles need to be cooled, because they are always on the verge of becoming *supercritical*—without water or some type of coolant, even uranium in a controlled chain reaction will overheat. When this occurs, the fuel rods melt and release the radioactive fission products trapped inside. This event is commonly called a *meltdown*. The *"China Syndrome"* sidebar below tells how this word was popularized. The explosion at Chernobyl is sometimes mistakenly called a meltdown. A true meltdown took place in the United States in 1979, at the Three Mile Island nuclear power

The China Syndrome

The accident at Pennsylvania's Three Mile Island caused people around the world to question the safety of nuclear plants. Such worries were further heightened by the release of a movie, *The China Syndrome,* in the spring of 1979. Ironically, the movie reached theaters at almost exactly the same time as the Three Mile Island accident.

The China Syndrome tells the story of a near-meltdown at a nuclear plant. While investigating the accident, a journalist realizes that an area "the size of Pennsylvania" had been threatened with annihilation. As the movie unfolds, plant management covers up the accident, and the journalist attempts to force the power company officials to admit that an accident had, in fact, occurred. This movie made the term *meltdown* a common—and often misunderstood—phrase in discussions about nuclear power.

Vincent Canby of the *New York Times* said of *The China Syndrome* that

> the film makes a compelling case based on man's not-so-rare predisposition to cut corners, to take the easy way out, to make a fast buck, to be lazy about responsibility, and to be awed by the authority representing vested interests. [The movie] is less about laws of [nuclear] physics than about public and private ethics.

station in Pennsylvania. At Three Mile Island, a loss of water allowed the fuel rods to partially melt. When engineers discovered the water loss, they pumped water from other sources into the reactor. This, in turn, caused that water to turn highly radioactive and allowed a small amount of radioactivity to escape into the atmosphere. The radioactive water leaked into a basement area in the reactor building, corroding the walls and floors and resulting in the need for major repairs.

The boron control rods in the reactor core are used to control the actual chain reaction. In most cases, temperature changes in the core are small and occur gradually. If technicians detect a sudden change in temperature, dropping all the control rods into the core, which causes all neutrons to be absorbed, can shut down a reactor. A shutdown of this type takes seconds and immediately ends the chain reaction. Inserting all the control rods into the core is called *scramming*.

A 47-year-old nuclear reactor gets repaired at Kiev's Institute for Nuclear Research in 1997. Since the accident at Chernobyl, Russian scientists are rigorous in their examination and repair of reactors. (Photo courtesy of Associated Press)

In a nuclear reactor, the core is usually placed inside an airtight, cylindrical, steel container that is located in a large reactor building built of concrete. Such structures are generally known as *containment buildings*. In case the fission process goes out of control and bursts the airtight cylinder, the thick walls and heavy roof of the building are supposed to prevent the release of radioactivity into the atmosphere.

In addition to using water as a cooling agent, the containment building also has a complex system of pipes to circulate the water from the core to the turbines. On its path, the hot, circulating water is sent to a heat exchanger that heats another water system to create steam. The steam drives the turbines. The water that condenses from the cooling steam is pumped back to the base of the core to help maintain a steady temperature.

Nuclear Accidents

In 1951 the first nuclear power plant was built to generate electricity. In more than 50 years since that first power plant, there have been thousands of instances in which radioactive wastes were accidentally released into soil, water, and air. Most of these incidents did not result in immediate injuries or massive environmental catastrophe. On the other hand, because the dangers of radioactivity may not be apparent for decades, it has been difficult for scientists to accurately assess the effects of nuclear power plant accidents. In addition to the 1979 Three Mile Island incident and the 1986 Chernobyl accident, nuclear scientists cite several other accidents at plants around the world as significant events.

The first major nuclear accident occurred on December 12, 1952, at the Chalk River reactor station near Ottawa, Canada. The event was a partial meltdown of the reactor's uranium fuel rods after an operator accident removed four control rods from the core. The reactor core was nearly demolished, and a large cloud of radioactive fallout was emitted. Millions of gallons of water inside the reactor became radioactive, but there were no injuries.

In November 1955, the first nuclear power plant built in the United States suffered a similar accident due to human error. An EBR-1 reactor in Idaho Falls, Idaho, suffered a partial core melt-down that destroyed it, with ensuing low-level contamination. There were no immediate injuries, but more than 100,000 gallons (378,400 l) of radioactive water leaked into the local water supplies.

On October 10, 1957, an accident occurred at the Windscale nuclear pile, north of Liverpool, England. This nuclear plant had a long history of minor safety problems, but the incident in 1957 was the most serious nuclear accident in the world to that time. Fire caused by human error resulted in 11 tons (9.9 mt) of uranium catching fire and the release of a cloud of radioactive smoke over a 200-square-mile (518-km²) area. The radioactive cloud traveled across the North Sea as far as Denmark. In London, England, 310 miles (500 km) from Windscale, radioactivity in the atmosphere was measured at 20 times the normal level after the fire.

No injuries were reported immediately after the incident. But radiation settled in farm fields surrounding the plant, and on October 12, British agricultural authorities banned all milk produced within over 190 square miles (500 km²) around the Windscale plant after October 10. More than 530,000 gallons (2 million l) of milk were poured into the rivers and sea because the milk was considered unsafe for human consumption. Despite the wide dispersal of radioactivity, a government report issued a month later stated that the accident had "no bearing on the safety of nuclear power stations being built for electricity authorities." The British Medical Research Council also announced that it was unlikely any harm had been done to human health.

Not until 1983 was a full-scale study released on the effects of the Windscale accident. According to the study, 32 people eventually died as a result of the fire at the Windscale pile. The toll also included 13 fatal cases of thyroid cancer and 260 other cases of

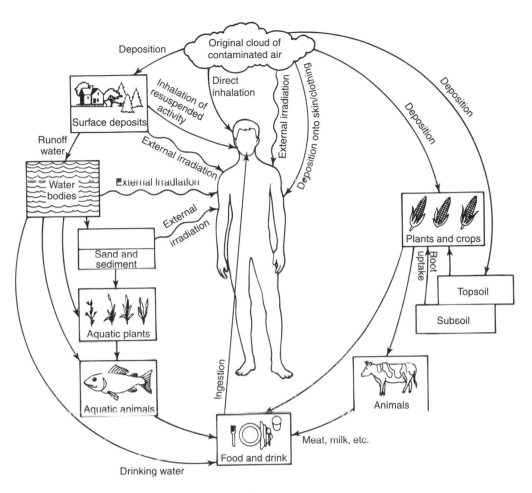

This diagram explains how radiation, when it affects soil or water, can lead to contamination of the entire food chain.

thyroid cancer that scientists attributed to the effects of the radioactive substance polonium released in the smoke.

In 1961 another major reactor accident in the United States occurred at Idaho Falls. An explosion occurred in a reactor room, the cause of which has never been determined. Three workers were killed instantly, and rescuers received high doses of radiation. The bodies of the three men killed were so severely irradiated that their exposed hands and heads had to be severed from their bodies and buried in a dump for radioactive waste.

The family of one victim, Army Specialist Richard McKinley, requested that he be buried in the Arlington National Cemetery in Arlington, Virginia. In order to accommodate the family's wishes, McKinley's commanding officer, Lieutenant Leon Monroe, had to send a special notice to Arlington authorities. His letter read in part: "Victim of nuclear accident. Body is contaminated with long-life radio-active isotopes. Under no circumstances will the body be moved from this location without prior approval of the Atomic Energy Commission in consultation with this headquarters."

In November 1975, an accident occurred at a nuclear plant near Leningrad in the Soviet Union. As in the later Chernobyl incident, Soviet authorities took great pains to withhold any information about the event. The accident resulted when a faulty tube in a reactor building ruptured, resulting in the release of a large cloud of radioactive iodine. Elevated readings of the substance were found as far away as 1,250 miles (2,000 km), yet the local population was never warned. There were no reports of injuries.

In 1989 an accident occurred at a nuclear power complex near Greifswald, Germany. The radioactive core of the reactor in the Greifswald plant nearly melted down due to a technical failure.

In 1999 an uncontrolled chain reaction at a power plant in Tokaimura, Japan, sent high levels of radioactive gas into the air. One worker was killed and two others seriously injured in Japan's worst nuclear accident.

Although the loss of life of nuclear plant workers has been much less than that of coal miners and oil field workers, past nuclear accidents have not been well publicized in the media at large. In most instances, no matter where the accident took place, government authorities went to great lengths to assure the public that there was no great danger.

CHAPTER 2

The Nuclear Community

The disaster at Chernobyl was the result of a period of several decades during which the Soviet Union, like other world powers, attempted to use nuclear power peacefully. By the late 1960s, the leadership of the Soviet Union had realized that the demand for electric power across the huge country was much greater than the government's ability to supply it.

The town of Pripyat, Ukraine, sits in the foreground of this picture of the Chernobyl nuclear power plant in November 2000. The plant was shut down in December 2000. (Photo courtesy of Associated Press)

One area where the demand for electricity was growing was Ukraine—in particular, the region around Kiev, its capital city. To meet this demand, in 1969, Soviet leaders decided that a nuclear power plant was needed. But finding an area near Kiev to build such an enormous plant was not easy.

South of the city, the Ukrainian plains stretched for thousands of miles. This was a region of fertile black soil that grew nearly enough grain to supply the entire nation. Plant construction there would damage agricultural production.

The area north of Kiev also presented problems. The region was largely a wilderness where the Pripyat River joined the Dnieper River—one of the largest rivers in the Soviet Union—and the Dnieper had been dammed to create a reservoir that supplied water to Kiev. The land in the region was known simply as the Pripyat Marshes—an enormous area of swamps, lakes, and scrub forests with sandy soil. The marshes made up one of the most remote areas of Ukraine, with few roads or railways for transportation of construction materials.

The decision was eventually made to build a power plant on a piece of land on the banks of the Pripyat River, about 13 miles (21 km) north of the old farming village of Chernobyl. In the early 1970s, construction was begun not only on two huge reactors and turbine buildings, but also on a new town to house workers and their families. In time, this town, only 1.2 miles (2 km) from the plant, would become known as Pripyat.

A Job with Many Requirements

By 1976, the first reactor at Chernobyl had been built at a cost of 100 million rubles (about $250 million), and a second was nearing completion. These reactors were the common Soviet nuclear reactors of that era, known as the RBMK. The need for nuclear power to generate electricity was so great, however, that Soviet engineers had increased the size of the reactors to massive dimensions.

The core of each reactor was an enormous mass of graphite weighing more than 2,500 tons (2,270 mt) that moderated the induced fission process. A maze of large holes, more than 1,600 in all, was drilled through the core for the placement of fuel-assembly tubes filled with uranium. Several hundred other holes served as tunnels for the raising and lowering of boron control rods. Each reactor was enclosed in a 30-story building covered by a concrete roof. Several hundred yards away were the turbine buildings, each of which housed two turbines that ran off one reactor.

Within the reactor building, six large pumps moved steam and boiling water from the core. The steam was forced through several hundred yards of pipe to the turbines, where electricity was generated. The water was then recirculated through the core to help cool it.

The person primarily responsible for managing the construction of the Chernobyl plant was 35-year-old Victor Brukhanov, a nuclear engineer. In addition to supervising the building of a mammoth nuclear power plant, he had to oversee the creation of an entire town.

As overwhelming as Brukhanov's responsibilities were, his task was complicated by another factor: the system of Soviet government. The Soviet Union was a one-party state dominated by the Communist Party. Membership in the party and unquestioning support of its goals were requirements for anyone who wanted to advance in any political, scientific, or military career.

At that time, a program known as the Five-Year Plan guided the Soviet Union's economy. Under the rule of Joseph Stalin in the 1930s, party leaders in Moscow had developed five-year plans without regard to whether their objectives could be achieved. Stalin died in 1953, but the Soviet practice of using five-year plans continued. If part of the plan called for a nuclear power plant to be built in Chernobyl in five years, that goal had to be met no matter what the costs. Those who failed to meet the schedule were often demoted or reassigned to less important positions.

For an engineer such as Brukhanov, the idea of meeting a schedule set hundreds of miles away by men who had no knowledge of nuclear power seemed foolish and dangerous. Nevertheless, to advance his career, Brukhanov met the deadline, but the quality of construction was shoddy and rushed in some of the structures within the plant's grounds.

Adding to the difficulties, the reactor design plans called for precision-made parts manufactured in industrial cities far from the remote Ukraine region. Because the Soviet Union was building so many reactors, parts were often supplied first to projects close to the manufacturing plants or to engineers who bribed party leaders and factory managers.

The Soviet nuclear industry's demand for parts was growing faster than the manufacturing could keep up with it, so there was competition among plant managers to obtain the required parts. A relatively young man such as Brukhanov had no connections in the party or with manufacturers, and as a result, he was forced to make some key parts such as valves, piping, and pumps for the Chernobyl reactors in workshops hastily built on the grounds of the plant. Such a "take-charge" attitude was widely admired by those under Brukhanov, and it helped them to meet their schedule. But his decision also meant that the reactors were built with parts that were not specifically approved by the original designers.

Another of Brukhanov's challenges was to attract enough workers to the wilderness around Chernobyl to staff the huge power plant. He took great pains to build Pripyat into a modern city that would attract the many specialists and workers needed to staff the plant. The new city was soon considered one of the prime locations for young workers in Ukraine and the surrounding area. Thanks to Brukhanov's planning, there were shopping centers, sports facilities, schools, and even an amusement park. Stores were well stocked with food and most were well supplied with goods that were difficult to get in other areas of the country.

In 1979, the reactor core at the Three Mile Island nuclear facility in Pennsylvania was severely damaged. In this photograph, George Kalman, right, a U.S. Nuclear Regulatory Commission engineer, has his breathing apparatus checked before entering the building a year later. (Photo courtesy of Associated Press)

The town soon had a population of more than 50,000. The average age of the residents was 26. These young Soviet citizens had come to Pripyat to work at the plant and to fill the many other occupations that were necessary to support the plant's workforce. Pripyat was ideal for young parents and their children. Housing was cheap, and necessities were plentiful. Forests that were ideal for hiking surrounded the town. The streams and lakes were filled with fish.

Only a mile from this ideal scene was one of the great marvels of Soviet technology—the V.I. Lenin power plant at Chernobyl. The first reactor opened in 1976, under the management of Brukhanov, who was widely admired by the workers of the plant and the citizens of Pripyat.

"Minor Accidents"

By 1978, a second reactor had been completed at Chernobyl, and plans were well under way for the completion of a third and fourth reactor by 1984. While Brukhanov was highly praised and workers were eager to move to the "paradise" at Pripyat, few realized that the massive RBMK reactors in use across the country had already malfunctioned at several plants.

Neither the government nor the Soviet press had reported the accidental release of a cloud of radioactive iodine at a power plant in the city of Leningrad three years earlier. This was the second time an accident had occurred there. Only 10 days after the second reactor went online at Chernobyl, a near-meltdown occurred in a nuclear reactor outside the city of Beloyarsk.

No news of any of these events was ever reported in the Soviet Union or in the world at large. Even nuclear engineers who might have learned how to correct flaws in the reactors, had they studied the accidents, were not informed.

Power plant workers at all levels firmly believed that Soviet reactors were safe. They were convinced that if they followed guidelines developed in the 1960s for much smaller reactors, they would be in no danger. Although power plant engineers were aware that what the Soviet energy ministry called "minor accidents" had occurred when pipes carrying the steam to the turbines had ruptured, the possibility of a major environmental catastrophe was never considered.

In March 1979, the nuclear accident at the Three Mile Island nuclear plant in the United States occurred. The accident was widely reported in news around the world. Many politicians and the press said that American companies cared more about profits than public safety. Soviet leadership, while concealing problems in Soviet plants, went to great length to publicly criticize the greedy American "capitalists." The "U.S. Government Action" sidebar on page 22 tells what measures the United States actually did take to regulate nuclear power.

Meanwhile, as more large RBMK reactors were put into service, it became apparent to those who worked with the enormous devices that there were problems that had never been addressed by Soviet political or scientific leadership. By the early 1980s, power

plant operators had found that running reactors for long periods on less than half power made them unstable. In such cases, a reactor might suddenly suffer a severe overheating of the core.

In cases of overheating, the normal emergency response in any nuclear plant was scramming, or dropping all the control rods into the core to stop the fission. But because the RBMK reactor core was so large, this action took much longer than it did on water-moderated reactors. In those reactors, scramming was completed in about four seconds. In the RBMK, it required between 18 and 20 seconds to insert all the control rods. As a result, a procedure that almost instantly smothered a chain reaction in the water-moderated reactors was much slower in the RBMK. The gap in time allowed the core to continue to heat. This, in turn, overheated the water in the cooling system, causing it to boil and explode in a matter of seconds.

Instead of improving the scramming procedure, which would have required a complete redesign, Soviet nuclear engineers

U.S. government leaders reacted with speed and were honest with the public regarding the 1979 nuclear accident at Three Mile Island in Pennsylvania, shown here. It still, however, ignited great interest and debate about the safety of nuclear power plants in this country. (Photo courtesy of Associated Press)

U.S. Government Action

The initial supervision of the U.S. nuclear power industry had been given to a group called the Atomic Energy Commission (AEC) in 1954. By the 1960s, however, critics claimed that some of the AEC's regulations were too weak. For example, an article in the magazine *Mother Earth News* noted, "According to many scientists…the AEC regulations on radioactive discharges from nuclear power reactors are far too tolerant for the safety of persons living in the vicinity…." As a result, Congress created the Nuclear Regulatory Commission (NRC) in 1974 to oversee nuclear issues regarding public health and safety.

After the accident at Three Mile Island, NRC scientists arrived at the plant within hours. Within two days, scientists had determined that there was no immediate danger to the surrounding area. To reassure the local population, NRC members requested that President Jimmy Carter come to the site, less than 100 miles (161 km) from the White House. The quick action of the NRC and the arrival of the president helped to defuse the crisis. The response of the NRC and U.S. leaders would later stand in stark contrast to Soviet actions after Chernobyl. Soviet leaders' first response was to stifle news of the accident and then downplay its severity.

arrived at a different solution for this problem. Their solution was to run reactors at full power all the time. This, not surprisingly, caused a great deal of wear on components such as steam pipes, welded joints, and moving parts. This wear problem surfaced at Chernobyl in 1981, when the plant's third reactor was brought into service. At that point, Brukhanov and his engineers decided to close down the first reactor for maintenance that was badly needed after five years of operation. The gradual process of reducing power in the enormous core required many hours and brought an unexpected result. The uranium in several of the fuel assemblies overheated, the way a car radiator might overheat in an idling car. Before control rods could be inserted, there was a slight explosion in the core, and a small amount of radiation was released into the atmosphere.

The event was a miniature preview of what would later occur on a massive scale. In this case, the emergency water-cooling system cooled down the reactor. There was no fire, and no one was injured except for several engineers who received high, but not fatal, doses of radiation.

Few people in Pripyat were aware of the event. The only clue that anything had happened came when crews from the plant hosed down the streets with water to "wash away" any fallout. The accident was so closely guarded that workers in the other two reactor buildings did not know that anything unusual had happened.

This extreme secrecy, coupled with the refusal to investigate possible design flaws, resulted in the failure to prepare for future problems. Instead, the party leadership was furious that one reactor at Chernobyl had to remain out of service for several months for repairs. This cost the government money, and orders came down from Moscow to fire several operators at the plant simply because they had been on duty when the accident occurred. This punishment made engineers even more reluctant to acknowledge any problems with the RBMK reactors.

Test at Reactor Four

On March 27, 1984, the fourth reactor was commissioned at the Chernobyl plant. Thanks to Brukhanov's management of the project, the reactor went into service three months ahead of schedule. This success drew major party leaders from Kiev, as well as the head of the Soviet Academy of Science, to the opening ceremony. Brukhanov received a bonus, and party leaders could now claim that the Lenin plant was generating enough electricity for all the homes and factories throughout the western Soviet Union. In fact, there was enough surplus electricity to give some to eastern European countries, such as Poland, that were *satellites*—under the economic and political control—of the Soviet Union.

Even as Reactor Four went online, the foundations for Reactors Five and Six were being poured. Within two years, according to the Five-Year Plan—which was renewed each year—Chernobyl would be the largest nuclear power plant in the world. But for Brukhanov, the praise of party leaders soon faded into renewed pressure. Not only were there schedule delays in Reactors Five and Six, but also the four reactors in operation endured a series of technical problems by 1986. Leaks in the air vents of the reactor buildings allowed radioactivity to escape. Leaks in the drains around the reactors' cores allowed as much as 3 cubic inches (50 cm³) of water to escape every hour, adding up to about 0.3 gallons (1.1 l) per day.

Party leaders as far away as Moscow were also pressuring Brukhanov. In late 1985, the leaders at the Ministry of Energy and Electrification, responding to a scientific study, ordered Brukhanov to immediately replace all roofs on the turbine buildings. But they did not tell him where he could find material for fireproof roofs 0.6 miles (1 km) long and 164 feet (50 m) wide.

Ministry inspectors at the plant also found that the cables in the reactor buildings did not have fireproof covers. Brukhanov explained that he was unable to get the covers, and the officials allowed the safety violation to remain.

In this atmosphere of pressure and hidden danger, Brukhanov depended a great deal on the supervisors directly under him. Among those that he relied upon the most was Anatoli Dyatlov, deputy chief engineer of Reactor Four. In early spring of 1986, overwhelmed with other problems, Brukhanov assigned Dyatlov to supervise Reactor Four during an important test.

Part of plant operations was to supervise an assessment of the turbines in case of a sudden loss of electric power. Such an event, should it occur in reality, would shut down all critical operations, including control rod motors and water-cooling systems in the reactor building. All plants had emergency generators to provide backup electricity. Nevertheless, it was important for plant safety to know

This 1986 photograph, taken at the Chernobyl nuclear power plant, shows the reactor's core cooling system. (Photo courtesy of REUTERS/Soviet Life/ Landov)

how much time would elapse between the loss of power to the turbines and the startup of power in the oil-powered generators.

In truth, the test was relatively simple. The test measured how long the turbines continued to spin—and provide power—after a sudden cut in electricity. Plant personnel under Brukhanov performed this test of the emergency electricity backup, but representatives of the Soviet Ministry of Energy and Electrification from Moscow also monitored it. In fact, the ministry considered the test so important that it was required before any reactor went online.

Brukhanov had been so eager to beat his deadline, however, that he had never run such a test on Reactor Four. For this reason, no one at the plant knew whether, or for how long, the turbines would operate the cooling water pumps or the control rod motors around the core if the power failed. Under normal circumstances, the turbines were supposed to spin from their own momentum for as long as a minute before the diesel-powered generators took over.

By late March 1986, word that the assessment had not been run on Reactor Four reached Moscow. In response, energy ministers decided to send a representative to conduct a test and report back. All that would be required of Brukhanov's crew—under Dyatlov—was to run Reactor Four on low power until signaled to switch it off. At that point, the turbines would be disconnected, and the energy representative would measure how long it took for the backup generator to engage.

The test was scheduled to take place in the last week of April 1986. Brukhanov was to be in Kiev at the time, as the sidebar "'What We Know Best'" relates below. Although he had never participated in such a safety test, Dyatlov agreed to supervise it. Like Brukhanov and most other engineers, he was unaware of the flaw in the RBMK reactor that caused a problem when it ran for any length of time at low power. This lack of information would play a key role as the Chernobyl disaster began to unfold.

"What We Know Best"

By 1986, the Soviet economy was in terrible shape. To bring more money into the government, party leaders in Moscow ordered all industrial enterprises—including power plants—to take steps to produce consumer goods.

In addition to his responsibility for the construction of two additional reactors at Chernobyl, Brukhanov was ordered to develop products to sell at Chernobyl. He was told that one power plant was producing aluminum plate engravings of famous events in Soviet history. The suggestion was even made to Brukhanov that he develop a small factory on the grounds to manufacture nuclear-powered meat grinders.

For Brukhanov, these ideas were absurd. "A nuclear power station is not a craft shop," he told his closest friends. "We [should] stick to what we know best and...generate electricity."

In the days leading up to the test at Reactor Four, Brukhanov was meeting with party leaders in Kiev. In addition to addressing plans for the new reactors, he was fighting demands that the power plant also build two large facilities on its grounds to store hay from farms in the surrounding region. The meeting kept him away from Chernobyl on April 24 and most of April 25.

CHAPTER 3

Fire and Confusion

The Chernobyl accident of April 1986 is generally regarded as the worst nuclear accident in history. The immediate blasts killed several workers, and exposure to radioactivity resulted in the deaths of dozens more within days or weeks. Most of those who received fatal doses of radioactivity were firefighters who responded to the alarm. Within hours, a cloud of dust carried by the wind exposed the people of Chernobyl, Pripyat, and Belarus to radioactivity 100 times greater than that from the Hiroshima bomb.

The destroyed reactor of the Chernobyl nuclear power plant is easily seen at the bottom of this 1986 photograph. (Photo courtesy of Associated Press)

Although 31 deaths are attributed to the actual event, studies in subsequent years have led to the conclusion that deaths and damage from the accident were long-term and far-reaching. By 1989, Soviet authorities admitted that more than 250 people who had worked at Chernobyl at the time of the explosion or participated in the cleanup had already died. The Soviet newspaper *Izvestia* wrote that same year that "many of those who worked a long time in conditions that were dangerous to their health need help today." In 2001 a report by the International Chernobyl Project, a charitable organization formed to support the "development of medical community and humanitarian aid programs that serve the [Chernobyl] region," stated that almost a quarter million people were still living on land so contaminated that they could not eat food grown on it. (Details of the media coverage of the Chernobyl disaster are found in Chapter 5.)

The Explosions

There is irony in the fact that the events leading to the worst nuclear power accident in history began with a safety test. The test of the backup power systems at the Chernobyl plant was scheduled for shortly after midnight on the morning of April 26, 1986. Since the surrounding communities had a low demand for electricity in the early morning hours, plant supervisors were confident that Chernobyl's other three nuclear reactors could handle all the electricity needs at that time.

At midnight, the new shift workers under their foreman, Alexander Akimov, entered the control room at Reactor Four. One of the workers was Leonid Toptunov, a nuclear engineer at the plant. Another plant engineer, Sasha Yuvchenko, was also nearby to observe the test.

Although most of these men had worked at the Chernobyl plant for years, few were familiar with the necessary emergency procedures should the reactor go out of control. Amazingly, in the rush to construct reactors and bring them online in accordance with the Five-Year Plan, there had never been an emergency drill held for the workers—not even a fire drill. But few workers felt worried about any mishaps. They believed that the country's nuclear industry was "accident-free." Only two months earlier, a power ministry official had stated in an interview that the odds of a nuclear accident occurring were "one in 10,000 years." In any case, he added, "the environment is also securely protected."

For almost 90 minutes, the engineers followed the procedure for lowering the energy generated by the reactor to the amount required for the test. When the approval was given, the power-generating turbines would be disconnected from the reactor. Engineers stationed elsewhere would then measure how long the giant turbines would continue to spin.

Unknown to the plant operators, the emergency alert system had been temporarily shut off in order to prevent it from responding to the test as if it were an accident. Such a response would cause the reactor to be flooded. But shutting off the alert system also disabled the pumps that sent water into the reactor's cooling system. By shortly after midnight, the water level in the cooling system had fallen to less than 1 percent capacity. This caused the reactor to overheat. Just before the turbines were disconnected, at about 1:20 A.M., Eastern European Summer Time (EEST), Toptunov saw that the energy level in the reactor was suddenly rising. He alerted Akimov, who immediately moved to completely shut down the reactor by reinserting the control rods to stop the fission process.

But it was too late. Even as the control rods were lowered, the temperature suddenly shot to almost 5,000°F (2,760°C)—100 times its normal level and twice the temperature needed to melt steel. Pressure in the pipes of the water-cooling system suddenly increased to more than 100 times the safe level. At 1:23 A.M. (EEST), the extreme pressure burst the cooling system pipes. That explosion was followed a split second later by another blast that destroyed the cylinder around the core and ripped the 1,000-ton (907-mt) roof off the reactor building.

Walls shook, lights flickered out, and powdery dust filled the room. Within seconds, tons of radioactive dust and debris shot up miles into the atmosphere. Large chunks of the graphite core shot out of the hole and began to burn as soon as they were exposed to air. These glowing—and highly radioactive—lumps of leadlike metal rained down on the grounds of the power plant, sparking more than 20 fires. The outside air rushing down into the building ignited the remaining graphite core.

The two explosions had destroyed Reactor Four. The worst release of radioactivity ever from a nuclear plant had just occurred.

Details of the Disaster

On April 25, the night before the explosions at the Chernobyl power plant, Alexander Akimov had been carrying out the instructions of deputy chief engineer Anatoli Dyatlov. He knew that the reduction of power in Reactor Four had to take place over a gradual period because of a side effect of the fission process. One of the by-products of the splitting of a uranium atom is the gas xenon. Like the element boron, xenon has the capacity to absorb neutrons without splitting. Reducing the fission too quickly ran the risk that excess xenon gas in the reactor would absorb neutrons at such a rate that the reactor would shut down. This would cause an immediate power blackout for millions of people in the region and would require restarting the entire chain reaction. Fortunately for the operation of nuclear power plants, xenon deteriorates, or decays, within a few hours. The rate of decrease in power had to occur gradually to allow time for the xenon to decay.

As the power declined over the next 12 hours, technicians had prepared to switch off Turbine Seven, one of two turbines powered by Reactor Four, when the reactor reached 50 percent of its power level. This step was necessary because running two large turbines off a reactor at half power was impossible. For the test to be done, therefore, Turbine Seven would be completely shut off, and the reactor would power the remaining turbine, Turbine Eight.

Power from the reactor would then be reduced to approximately 30 percent. At this point, the second turbine could be switched off, and engineers could measure how long the turbine blades spun before stopping. Standards required that turbine blades spin between 45 and 50 seconds to allow time for a backup generator to be started. If the measurements did not meet the required amount of time, leaving the reactor at 30 percent power would allow technicians to reconnect the turbine, power it up, and repeat the test.

By 2:00 P.M. (EEST) on April 25, Turbine Seven had been completely disconnected from the reactor. Engineers were ready to reduce power to 30 percent and test Turbine Eight. At that point, Dyatlov, who had not supervised such tests before, realized

This diagram illustrates the process that creates power inside an RBMK reactor.

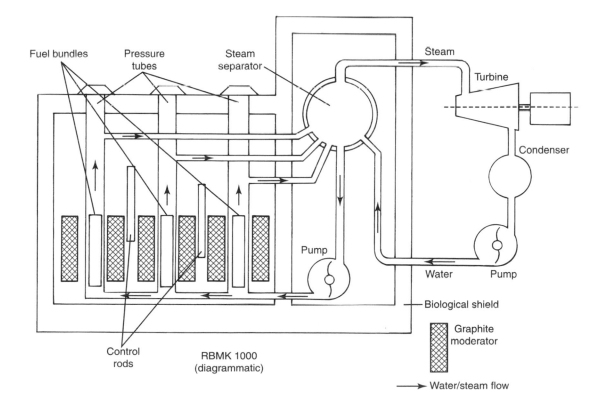

that completely shutting off both turbines was a problem. Such an action would decrease the water flowing between the turbines and the reactor. In addition, if the test were not performed within a specified amount of time and the turbines reconnected, the backup generators actually would start. This combination—a reduced water flow and a generator startup—would activate the emergency alert system and send a computerized signal to the automatic cooling system that an accident had occurred. The signal would trigger an immediate flooding of the reactor. Because he was impatient to complete the test and resume full operations, Dyatlov gave permission to disconnect the emergency alert system while the test was being performed.

All was ready for the test when a call came from the Ministry of Energy in Kiev. Engineers there said that power was needed in the region, so Turbine Eight would have to be operated until

Engineer Sergey Bashtovoi turns the key of the emergency stop as the Chernobyl nuclear power plant's last working reactor is disabled. The official closing of the plant occurred on December 15, 2000. (Photo courtesy of Associated Press)

11:00 P.M. (EEST). The test was then postponed, but the reactor was not brought to full power. Instead, it continued to run at slightly less than half power for the rest of April 25.

At midnight, Dyatlov and his crew returned to attempt the test once again. Permission had come from Kiev to disconnect Turbine Eight. Akimov, Toptunov, and others, including engineer Sasha Yuvchenko, prepared to oversee reactor functions while the outside engineers ran the test.

Both Akimov and Toptunov were uneasy, however. With the emergency system switched off, their only reading came from a single computer printout across the large control room from the operating panel. For the men managing the reactor, the most critical information was the number of control rods that were in the core to control the fission process.

For Toptunov, who was at the main controls of Reactor Four, the challenge in reducing power was to balance the insertion of control rods with the natural neutron absorption of the xenon gas. This was made more difficult by the shutting off of the auto matic emergency alert system that would have notified operators of an excessive drop in power. As a result, at 12:30 A.M. (EEST) on April 26, the computer printout showed that the reactor had fallen to less than 5 percent power. Xenon gas was filling the reactor building, accelerating the shutdown. This indicated that the test should be abandoned and the reactor shut down completely until all systems could be examined for any damage.

Dyatlov ignored the suggestions of Toptunov and Akimov to cancel the test. He was anxious to get the procedure finished and return the reactor to full service. He ordered Toptunov to immediately withdraw seven of the remaining 18 control rods in the core to increase the power. Thus, there were now only 11 of a total of 211 control rods actually in the core. By 1:20 A.M. (EEST), the power had risen to a level sufficient to run the test.

The flaws in the RBMK reactor were not widely known at the time. The fact that the reactor had been operating at generally low power for more than 12 hours was of no concern. But the extended period of low-power operation meant that the normal water-cooling process was working more slowly than it should have been working. Under normal circumstances, this slowdown would have been registered automatically, but the emergency override prevented that information from reaching the control room.

At 1:23 A.M. (EEST), Dyatlov gave the go-ahead for the turbine test. As he did, Toptunov saw that the power in the reactor had begun to rise rapidly. He shouted to Akimov that the reactor was heating up too fast. Akimov, in turn, told Dyatlov that he was going to reactivate the emergency switch and lower all control rods into the core at once. But it required between 18 and 20 seconds to insert all the control rods into an RBMK reactor. At this point the rods could not be reinserted quickly enough to create an emergency shutdown.

A rumble that seemed to rise from deep within the reactor building suddenly shook the control room. Akimov looked at the computer printouts, which showed that the control rods had stopped their descent. He immediately pulled a switch to allow them to fall of their own weight into the core. A split second later, an earthquake-like shudder shook the control room, and the lights flickered out.

At the moment the second explosion hit, Yuvchenko was getting supplies in a storeroom down the hall from the control room. The force of the blast threw him to the floor. In the darkness, he heard a groan. "What happened?" a voice said in the darkness.

"I don't know," called out Yuvchenko. "It may be war." Grabbing a flashlight, he made his way into a hallway that led to the reactor building. The engineer bumped into a man there whose face was covered with blisters and blood. The injured man pointed to the reactor building and groaned through blistered lips that several men were trapped there. Making his way into the enormous 30-story structure, Yuvchenko could not believe his eyes. There was nothing over his head but the star-filled night sky.

He realized that the concrete roof of the reactor containment building had been blown off.

Like most people in the moments after the blast, Yuvchenko was uncertain exactly what had occurred. From the road outside the power station, he could see the full scope of the disaster. Half of the fourth reactor building's roof was gone. Moving closer, he looked through a hole in the side of the structure into the area of the building that had held the core. All he could see was a strange glow, as if he were looking down into a volcano, but he was actually looking at exactly what nuclear experts had warned about—a graphite core fire.

Firefighters Respond

Inside the control room, Dyatlov, Akimov, and Toptunov studied the gauges on the control panels. They knew that a major catastrophe had occurred. Although the explosion was not a nuclear blast—nothing would have been left of the plant had that been the case—there was a clear danger that radioactivity was escaping into the surrounding area and into the atmosphere.

Dyatlov had worked with reactors for more than 20 years and had assisted in the construction of Reactor Four. Ordering the other two men to call firefighters and remain at the control panel, Dyatlov ran to the reactor area. As Yuvchenko had seen, an eerie glow came from deep in the reactor floor where the core had once been. Torn electrical wires hung down from the walls. Water from ruptured pipes poured onto the cables, sending waterfalls of sparks into the thick smoke that filled the cavernous area.

Minutes passed, and Dyatlov heard the sirens of approaching fire engines. Dyatlov made his way outside to direct firefighters to the nearest water hydrants. As he walked across the grounds, he saw smoking lumps of what appeared to be graphite. This confirmed his worst nightmare. Portions of the core had been blown apart. The glow coming from the reactor was a core fire. If the fire was not contained, the uranium fuel assembly was in danger of total meltdown.

Meanwhile, Lieutenant Leonid Pravik and a firefighting unit from Pripyat had arrived and were now positioned high on what was left of the roof of Reactor Building Four. They were not attempting to put out the fire there, but were instead aiming their hoses at the roof of Reactor Building Three, where red-hot chunks of graphite had started several small fires. Although Pravik and his men were experienced firefighters, they had never faced such intense heat. The flames were hot enough to vaporize steel, and the remains of the roof began melting under their feet.

A radioactive accident was always a possibility at a nuclear power station, but there had been no preparations at the plant or in the community for such an emergency. In the minds of Soviet officials, to prepare for disaster was an admission that one could occur. This went against the Communist Party's prevailing attitude.

The Chernobyl Memorial stands in memory of the 31 firefighters who lost their lives while fighting the fires at the Chernobyl nuclear power facility. (Photo courtesy of Peter Turnley/CORBIS)

None of Pravik's men was wearing special protective clothing or masks to prevent exposure to radiation. By 3:00 A.M. (EEST), the firefighters, as well as many of the shift workers at Reactor Four, were feeling the effects of radiation poisoning. They became dizzy and nauseated. Some began to vomit. Others remarked on a strange taste in their mouths, a combination of metal and chocolate.

By 4.00 A.M. (EEST), firefighting units from surrounding towns, including Chernobyl and even Kiev, had arrived to support the Pripyat crew. By dawn, most of the graphite fires scattered around the grounds of the plant had been extinguished. The main reactor fire, however, was burning out of control. Smoke from the fire continued to spew radioactive fallout into the air. Pravik and some of his men were so weak by this time that they had to be evacuated. As he left the grounds of the plant, Pravik recognized a man entering the gates—Chernobyl's director, Victor Brukhanov.

"I Am Not Joking"

Brukhanov had spent most of the previous two days in Kiev. He had met with party leaders and energy ministers to discuss the lack of progress in the construction of Reactors Five and Six. Returning to Pripyat late on April 25, Brukhanov was awakened at about 2:00 A.M. (EEST) the next morning by a call from the power plant. "Some sort of accident, something really bad, has happened at the fourth unit," said the caller.

Brukhanov was on his way to the plant in minutes. As he passed through the main gates, he could see that the roof had been blown off Building Four. Going directly to the control room, Brukhanov found Dyatlov and Akimov. Neither man could explain what had happened. Both, in fact, assured Brukhanov that the reactor was in working order. (Due to radiation sickness, Akimov was later replaced by another foreman at the plant, as described in the "One in Ten Million" sidebar on page 38.)

"One in Ten Million"

A few hours after the blast, engineer Anatoli Dyatlov peered through the dust outside the control room and saw that his shift foreman, Alexander Akimov, was beginning to suffer the effects of the heat and radiation. He ordered a call to Pripyat for a replacement.

The call went to Vladimir Babichev, the foreman scheduled to come on at dawn. Like many workers at the plant, Babichev had been trained to believe that the reactors were safe. Although his eyes told him that there had been a catastrophe, he did not believe he was in danger. Babichev did not bother to wear a mask or protective boots. Forcing his way to the control room, he found Akimov.

"What happened?" asked Babichev.

Akimov shook his head. "During the test there was an explosion. We don't know what went wrong."

"I seem to remember you saying that the odds of an accident were one in ten million," said Babichev.

"Yes...and this seems to be it," replied Akimov.

Brukhanov realized then that his closest assistants were in a condition of shock. He became even more alarmed when he asked a health worker that he encountered to take a reading of the radioactivity in the atmosphere. The instruments measured radioactivity in units called *rems*. A reading of 3.6 rems was considered high. The health worker told Brukhanov that the needle went off the dial at 250 rems. In other words, most of the people in the building and on the grounds had received deadly doses of radiation. (More about rems can be found in the "Measurements of Radioactivity" sidebar on page 39.)

Brukhanov began to make phone calls to various party officials from Kiev all the way to Moscow. Although he could not explain precisely what had happened, the news of the radiation reading was enough to send the message to the highest levels of Soviet government that a disaster had occurred at Chernobyl.

Brukhanov made his final call as dawn approached. He reached the official in charge of the Communist Party in Pripyat. Brukhanov said that preparations should be made to evacuate the city.

"You must be joking," the official said. "An evacuation will cause mass panic."

"I assure you I am not joking," replied Brukhanov. He knew that an evacuation would cause more than panic. An evacuation would break the Soviet law that all nuclear accidents were to remain state secrets. Moving

50,000 people was such an enormous task that it would alert the entire world to the disaster at Chernobyl. On the other hand, he realized, not to evacuate the city would be to condemn thousands of his fellow citizens to sickness and possible death. Before anyone at Pripyat had to make a final decision, Brukhanov received word from Moscow that scientists and party ministers would arrive at the plant by noon. No action was to be taken until then.

In Pripyat, townspeople began the day—Saturday—as usual. At about noon, less than 12 hours after the blast, one resident came inside after sunning himself on his apartment roof. He cheerfully noted that he had never tanned so quickly. Within hours, he was taken to the hospital, vomiting uncontrollably. He would die a painful death within weeks from a fatal dose of radioactivity.

Many of Pripyat's residents were soon coughing, vomiting, and complaining of a metallic taste in their mouths. The radioactivity from Chernobyl had begun to spread.

Measurements of Radioactivity

Radioactivity was first discovered in the early 1900s. The amount of radioactivity given off by substances such as uranium was measured in *roentgens*. These units of measurement are named after Wilhelm Roentgen, the man who discovered X-rays—radioactive rays similar to gamma rays.

As scientists investigated further, they discovered radioactivity's harmful effects on humans. At that point, scientists developed a measurement known as a *rad* (radiation absorbed dose). More research revealed the different types of radioactive rays, as well as the fact that each ray had different biological effects on humans. The measurement for these effects was called a rem (roentgen equivalent, man). One rad of gamma radiation was equivalent to one rem, while one rad of alpha radiation equaled 20 rems. At the time of the Chernobyl disaster, rads and rems were the common measurements.

Since then, scientists have developed the terms *gray* (Gy) and *sievert* (Sy). One gray is equivalent to 100 rads, and 1 sievert is equal to 100 rems.

CHAPTER 4

The Catastrophe Unfolds

Workers wearing inadequate protection sift through the rubble of the accident and ensuing fire that occurred in Reactor Four of the Chernobyl plant. (Photo courtesy of dpa/Landov)

By dawn, almost four and a half hours after the explosion in Reactor Four, all of the graphite fires on the grounds of the plant had been put out. The only fire remaining to be extinguished was the graphite core fire inside the reactor structure. Unfortunately, firefighting crews did not know what to do about this blaze. They continued to fight it the only way they knew how—by pouring water into the massive hole. This did nothing but create enormous clouds of radioactive steam that blew northwest toward Pripyat.

In all, more than 30 crews totaling nearly 200 firefighters battled the fires. Many of these men suffered severe burns from the flames, and most, if not all, suffered serious radiation exposure.

By 6:30 A.M. (EEST), while authorities in Moscow were preparing to come to Chernobyl, many of the workers on the overnight shift in other reactor units at the plant were also suffering extreme reactions to radiation poisoning.

The Effects of Radiation Exposure

Hearing of the disaster, Andrei Belokon, a doctor at Pripyat's only hospital, rushed to the plant to administer first aid to injured workers and firefighters. More than 100 cots were set up in a room at the plant, and most of the severely injured victims were treated there first before being evacuated to the hospital at Pripyat, where a radiation burn quarantine unit was being set up. But upon his arrival at the power station, Dr. Belokon discovered that the first-aid station and medical supply room were closed. No nurse or other health care provider was on duty. Belokon saw that many of the plant workers were so severely burned that blistered skin hung loosely on their limbs, nearly slipping off. There was little he could do for these people. In an interview several years after the disaster, Belokon described a worker about 18 years old who needed medical attention.

> They brought in a chap…complaining of nausea and [a] severe headache, and he had begun vomiting. [He] worked in the third reactor and, it seems, had gone to the fourth…. I took his blood pressure. It was 140 or 150 over 90, a little high. Then it rose quickly and the chap became delirious…. I took him to the first-aid section…but there was nowhere even to sit. The medical room was shut. I took him to the ambulance. He became delirious before my very eyes…he showed symptoms of confusion, couldn't speak and began to mumble as if he'd had a drink or two, although he didn't smell of alcohol. He was very pale. It was already too late.

By morning, the men who had been in the control room—Dyatlov, Akimov, Toptunov, and 15 other staff members—were dizzy and vomiting. By that time, a shuttle bus was transporting the injured to the hospital in Pripyat. In all, more than 120 workers were shuttled from the plant to the hospital.

Dr. Anatoli Ben, another doctor at Pripyat's hospital, had been tending to the victims of burns and radiation poisoning since before dawn. At 5:00 A.M. (EEST), Yuvchenko was brought in, complaining of nausea and a strange taste in his mouth. Ben observed deep radiation burns on Yuvchenko's arms and became concerned that he might have to amputate them.

"How do you feel?" Ben asked.

"Fine. A little dizzy," Yuvchenko answered.

Although he wanted to go home, Yuvchenko was highly radioactive. Like the others in the vicinity of the blast, he was assigned to the large dormitory area on the top floor of the hospital, where he received an intravenous drip of fluids and antibiotics to fight infection. Like most burn victims who have lost large amounts of skin, Yuvchenko was vulnerable to infection. What he did not understand was Ben's greatest fear for all the victims: radiation in large doses destroys the tissues of the lungs and intestines. (Citizens in the area thought they knew ways to prevent radiation sickness from worsening by using common household foods and drinks, as the "Folk Remedies" sidebar describes on page 43.)

Keeping the Secret

In his office at the plant, Brukhanov was still trying to determine what had happened. He was also trying to determine a way to keep news of the accident from spreading. Meanwhile, Soviet troops arrived and circled the plant to keep out any observers.

Despite the ambulances and shuttles carrying injured and ill workers to Pripyat, few of the city's residents were aware that anything had happened overnight. The day was a beautiful, warm, spring day, and there was no outward sign of a disaster. Children went to their usual half-day of school on Saturday. Those too young for school played outside. Gardeners worked on their plots, unaware that the plants they were tending were covered with radioactive fallout.

At midmorning, the exhausted Ben looked out the window of the hospital. He saw people sunbathing. Others were fishing in the river that ran through the town and past the plant. Finally, when Ben saw a wedding party at an outdoor café, he left the hospital to warn the party about the danger. The group thanked him and went on with their celebration.

Soviet officials in town tried to dismiss the accident. When questioned about what appeared to be smoke coming from the plant, an official remarked, "It was a steam discharge from the power plant. Aren't you used to that?"

Folk Remedies

As word of the disaster began to filter into Pripyat, the families of those who had been taken to the hospital rushed to check on their condition. Many of the workers who had received large doses of radiation were exhibiting few outward symptoms other than dizziness and a metallic taste in their mouths. Nevertheless, they were quarantined because they were dangerously radioactive.

Few of the people of Pripyat, however, realized the hazards they faced. In fact, because the Soviet government had gone to great lengths to assure nuclear workers about the safety of nuclear power, many people believed that radiation poisoning could be cured with simple folk remedies.

As a result, many of the people brought cucumbers, fresh milk, and mineral water to the hospital. Eating the vegetables or drinking the milk or water was widely believed to cure radiation poisoning. Another widely accepted remedy was vodka. In fact, a nurse supplied 1.8 ounces (50 gm) of vodka each to many of the firefighters. Although most claimed to feel better initially, they soon became ill from the effects of alcohol and radiation.

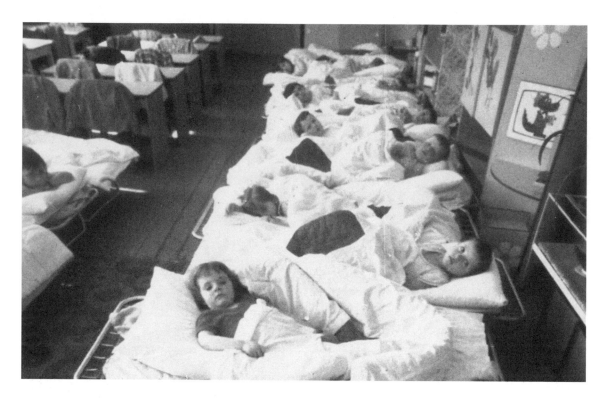

In 1990, these children were photographed in a clinic in Syekovo, Ukraine, not far from the town of Chernobyl. Many children in the region suffer from intestinal problems and other sicknesses due to radiation exposure from the 1986 nuclear accident. (Photo courtesy of Associated Press)

Lyubov Lelechenko, the wife of one of the plant workers, slept soundly through the night of the accident. When she woke up late the next morning, her mother said that she had heard strange sounds coming from the power station during the night. In an interview several years after the event, Lelechenko described what she had seen when she went outside.

> I saw a policeman here, another there; I had never seen so many policemen in the town. They weren't doing anything, just sitting in various places, at the post office, the Palace of Culture.... Yet people were walking about normally, there were children everywhere. It was very hot. People were going to the beach... or sitting by the stream.... Anya, my daughter, had already gone to school. I had to go shopping, but I told my mother, "I don't know what has happened, but when Anya returns from school, take her straight into the house."

I went back to the central [market]…and the reactor was quite visible…it was burning and its wall was broken. There were flames above the hole. That chimney between the third and fourth [reactors]…looked like a burning column.…Nobody said anything. Well, they said there was a fire. But about radiation, that radioactivity was escaping, there was not a word. Anya came back from school and said, "Mama, we had physical exercise outside for almost a whole hour." It was insanity.

"The Worst the World Has Ever Known"

Brukhanov spent much of the early hours after the accident reassuring party leaders and nuclear specialists in Moscow that everything was under control. Nevertheless, as soon as military units arrived, reports indicated that a major catastrophe had occurred. Civil defense alerts were spread among civilian units across the western regions of the Soviet Union.

Word spread quickly among scientists who were experts in the field of nuclear energy. Among the scientists in Moscow, one of those most concerned was Valeri Legasov, the first deputy director of the Kurchatev Institute, the Soviet nuclear power commission. Legasov was considered a leading Soviet expert on nuclear power and on the RBMK reactors.

Throughout the morning of April 26, Legasov received reports in his office. With each new bit of information, he became increasingly worried. Finally, at noon, he called his wife to say that he was flying immediately to Ukraine. His wife asked for more details about the sudden change in his usual schedule. "There has been a terrible accident at Chernobyl," he said. "The worst the world has ever known."

Legasov and his panel of nuclear experts did not reach Pripyat until the early evening of April 26. They were briefed on what was known at that point. An explosion had destroyed the containment building of Reactor Four and ignited the graphite core. The roof had been blown to one side, leaving the reactor open to the atmosphere. After the briefing, the scientists flew over the site by helicopter, swooping as close as safety would allow to the shattered reactor building.

Legasov determined that fission in the reactor had ceased. The glow that could be seen was in fact burning graphite that was sending huge amounts of radioactivity into the air. Legasov knew that graphite burned at a rate of about 1 ton (0.9 mt) per hour. The core in Reactor Four contained 2,500 tons (2,270 mt) of graphite. This meant that it could take more than three months for the fire to burn out.

As serious as that problem was, Legasov realized that the accident presented an even graver threat. If the temperature of the burning graphite increased, there was a danger that the uranium

The deserted town of Pripyat, which used to be home to 50,000 people, now stands abandoned and guarded by soldiers who enforce an 18-mile (29-km) restriction zone around Chernobyl because of the ever-present aftereffects of radiation exposure. (Photo courtesy of Associated Press)

itself would melt. This could result in the most nightmarish of all possibilities—a meltdown of radioactive material deep enough into the earth to reach the underground water table and poison the water for millions of square miles.

There was also a third potential danger. Up to this point, firefighters had been pouring water on the core. This had only created more clouds of radioactive steam. At about 4,500°F (2,500°C), Legasov knew, water itself would separate into its explosive components, oxygen and hydrogen. Therefore, dropping water on the fire could actually cause an explosion, worsening the already disastrous situation.

After the helicopter tour, Legasov explained that the only solution was to smother the fire with sand mixed with boron to absorb neutrons. The assembled managers and scientists were astonished when the chief scientist told them that, according to his calculations, it would require almost 4,000 tons (3,630 mt) of sand to smother the enormous burning core. When the group protested that such a task was almost impossible, Legasov reminded them that the blast had created two serious sources of radioactive danger. The first was a cloud rising from the reactor and drifting north over Pripyat, carrying levels of radioactivity 10 times above that considered safe. The second danger came from the debris and dust scattered by explosion. This was composed of graphite, other metals, concrete, and even microscopic bits of uranium. As long as the fire continued to burn, the poison would spread on the wind. The devastation would be incalculable.

Legasov and his colleagues now faced two critical tasks. The first was relatively simple. They ordered all reactors at Chernobyl to be shut down until the fire in Reactor Four was contained. The second task was assembling a helicopter fleet and workers to undertake the enormous job of smothering the fire. Not only would the project require an enormous number of machines and workers, but also news of the event would be passed among the population. Orders were given to assemble as many helicopters as possible and recruit laborers to begin loading them with sand to be dropped onto the core. At most, a helicopter could carry 100 tons (91 mt) of sand. Delivering 4,000 tons of sand would require 40 helicopter trips, at the least.

Next, officials had to decide whether or not to evacuate Pripyat. By now, the dawn of April 27 was approaching. The core fire had been burning for more than 24 hours. Many residents were increasingly suspicious that a catastrophe had occurred far beyond what was being announced. By early morning, thousands had already left the city. Many of those who remained were showing signs of radiation sickness. Throughout the previous day, civil defense workers in Kiev had assembled nearly 800 buses, 300 cars, and two trains. They were gathered around the city in a state of alert.

At noon on April 27, after people had been exposed to excessively dangerous levels of radiation for almost 36 hours, Soviet military commanders gave the order to evacuate. Over loudspeakers and on radio, residents were told to pack only one bag with enough clothing for three days. Many in Pripyat, however, suspected that they would never return.

That afternoon, the entire remaining population of Pripyat—30,000 people—was evacuated in a little more than three hours. The 1,100 vehicles from Kiev took the residents of Pripyat to temporary lodging in what was considered to be a safe zone 20 miles (32 km) from the plant. As the long lines of buses carried citizens out of Pripyat, helicopters loaded with sand flew overhead. Their destination was the still-burning core of Reactor Four.

In the following days, as readings of radioactive fallout increased outside the safe zone, authorities outlined a wider ring of safety. The evacuees from Pripyat were moved once again, along with about 100,000 other people whose towns, villages, and farms were located within a 30-mile (48-km) radius of the power plant. They were also told to pack enough clothing for three days, but they never returned to their homes.

CHAPTER 5

"A Danger We Cannot See"

Despite the monumental nature of the events over the weekend of April 26 and 27, the world at large knew virtually nothing about the disaster at Chernobyl. This was the result of several factors. First, Brukhanov had followed the standard Soviet protocol for any accident. He did all in his power to reassure party leaders in Kiev and Moscow that the problem at Chernobyl was minor. At the same time, militia and civil defense personnel sealed off the entire area around the plant. These people had only been told that there had been a fire at the plant.

In a nation as immense as the Soviet Union, the vast majority of Soviet citizens knew nothing about the events, but this was due more to government control than to lack of information. On

Alexander Lovalenko, information chief of the Chernobyl cleanup, stands in front of the aban doned Chernobyl nuclear power plant. He holds up a radia- tion meter indicating that the level of radia- tion currently in the air is hundreds of thousands of times less than in the days immediately following the accident. (Photo courtesy of REUTERS/Meg Bortin/Landov)

Sunday, April 27, Soviet leaders prohibited the editors of the government newspaper *Izvestia* from publishing a news report providing details of the accident.

As the government struggled to prevent news of the Chernobyl disaster from spreading, the radiation from the blast itself spread quickly. Carried by strong winds, a huge radioactive cloud moved northwest, raining radioactive particles over millions of square miles. The areas affected went far beyond the borders of Ukraine. The nearby Soviet republics of Belarus, Russia, and Georgia received high amounts of fallout. Countries in eastern and northern Europe, including Poland, Sweden, Finland, and Norway, were also in its path. Even distant countries such as the United States and Japan would eventually receive measurable amounts of radioactive fallout, although at levels far lower than those measured in Pripyat.

The deadly cloud carried by the prevailing winds contained vaporized graphite and uranium fuel. By-products of nuclear fission called isotopes, which form when uranium atoms are split, were also carried along. Within two days of the explosion, *plutonium*—one of the most poisonous elements known to humans—was drifting over millions of unsuspecting people. Other dangerous by-products, much more radioactive than uranium or plutonium, included iodine-131, strontium-90, and cesium-13.

Alert in Sweden

By April 28, 1986—more than 48 hours after the Chernobyl blasts—researchers in Sweden began to suspect that there had been a core meltdown in the Ukraine area. Early on that Monday morning, nuclear technicians at the Forsmark Nuclear Power Plant, 60 miles (96 km) north of Stockholm, Sweden, received warning signals at their monitoring stations. The readings indicated extremely high levels of radiation—a sure sign of serious trouble.

At first, the Swedish technicians feared a problem in the Forsmark reactors and began emergency procedures to check all operations. When all reactors were gauged to be operating safely, the technicians used Geiger counters to test more than 600 workers at the plant for exposure. (A *Geiger counter* is a device that measures radiation.) Again, they were alarmed—radioactive readings from the workers' clothing far exceeded contamination levels. Geiger counter readings of the soil and greenery surrounding the plant also showed four to five times the normal amount of radioactive emissions. Obviously, a major nuclear catastrophe had occurred, but no one knew where or when.

The technicians at Forsmark were the first people—but by no means the only people—to pick up readings of excessive radioactivity in the atmosphere. To the northeast, spring snow was falling over parts of Finland. From there to Norway and Denmark to the southwest, the same ominous readings were soon detected. Somewhere, nuclear experts agreed, an enormous amount of radioactivity was entering the atmosphere and, even worse, settling on people, plants, and animals. A thorough check of all pos-

Radiation from the Chernobyl nuclear accident traveled across Europe, settling on land, people, and animals. In this photograph, scientists test the radiation levels of vegetables in a region of Ukraine close to the accident. (Photo courtesy of dpa/Vetter/Landov)

sible sources in Sweden led to a horrifying suspicion. There had been a meltdown in the neighboring Soviet Union.

Meteorologists examining the wind patterns verified the fears of many people. Throughout the weekend, high-altitude air currents had been blown northwest from the Black Sea, across Ukraine, over the Baltic states, and into Scandinavia. If there had been an accident, the winds were now carrying radioactive particles into other countries. Nevertheless, when members of the Swedish scientific community insisted on April 28 that there had been a major accident of some kind, the Soviets denied any knowledge of such an event.

A Challenge to Glasnost

For Soviet premier Mikhail Gorbachev, the disaster at Chernobyl could not have come at a worse time. Gorbachev had been in office only 13 months when the explosion occurred. He had come to power with the support of many in the Soviet Union who were tired of the economic failure and high-level corruption under the Communist system. Gorbachev had won wide public support for a policy he called *glasnost*—the Russian word for "openness." Not only was Gorbachev popular with the Soviet people, but Western political leaders had also warmly received him. His relative youth and health in comparison to former Soviet leaders, as well as his stated desire to change Soviet politics and society, created an optimism about international relations that had not existed for many years.

Unfortunately for the Soviet people, there was little that one man—even one with such popular support as Gorbachev—could do to change the Soviet political system quickly. The premier had assumed power over an inefficient, aging, corrupt state bureaucracy that was determined to fight glasnost and remain as closed as it had always been. When news of Chernobyl reached Moscow, Gorbachev was caught between two opposing points of view.

Many old-style political officials were reluctant to open up the Soviet Union to criticism from other nations that had long been enemies. This reluctance, and the government's total control of internal matters, were responsible for the delay in publicly reporting the accident and the nearly two days that elapsed before the evacuation of the affected area.

On the other hand, Gorbachev and supporters of his new policies realized that maintaining secrecy went against glasnost. Hiding such a disaster as Chernobyl would not solve the problem, which seemed to be beyond the capabilities of Soviet nuclear authorities.

After several days of debate among factions of the Soviet leadership, it was agreed that a brief announcement would be made to the Soviet people. Finally, therefore, at 9:00 P.M. (EEST) on Monday, April 28, the Soviets announced the accident on national television. A newscaster on Moscow television read a four-sentence statement from the Council of Ministers. The brief announcement said in full: "An accident has taken place at the Chernobyl power station, and one of the reactors was damaged. Measures are being taken to eliminate the consequences of the accident. Those affected by it are being given assistance. A government commission has been set up."

The flat, almost expressionless announcement at the end of the national news raised as many questions as it answered. This was especially true in areas of Europe directly in the path of the "consequences." On Tuesday, a ham (amateur) radio operator in the Netherlands reported receiving a message from a ham operator near Chernobyl. According to the Dutch operator, the Soviet contact claimed that a reactor was burning and that "many hundreds" were "dead and wounded." According to the Dutch report, the Soviet operator said, "We heard heavy explosions! You can't imagine what's happening here....I'm here 20 miles [32 km] from it, and in fact I don't know what to do. I don't know if our leaders know what to do because this is a real disaster. Please tell the world to help us."

Without any detailed information from the Soviet government, this unconfirmed report was widely carried by the international media, including the nightly news broadcasts in the United States. In spite of this frightening radio contact, Soviet officials hesitated to ask for outside help for fear of revealing the true extent of the disaster at Chernobyl.

On Tuesday morning, April 29, a science specialist from the Soviet embassy in Bonn, West Germany, appeared unannounced and without an appointment at the Bonn office of the Atomforum, an agency in charge of West Germany's nuclear power operations. The Soviet official asked the scientists at Atomforum if the Germans could advise his country on the best methods for extinguishing a graphite fire, and specifically if anyone in Germany knew how to put out a graphite fire in a nuclear reactor core. A similar behind-the-scenes request was made the same day to the Swedish nuclear authority.

Despite this ominous request, the Soviets continued to refuse to discuss exactly what had happened at Chernobyl. The Soviet official who sought West German help said almost nothing about the reason for his request. At last, a West German scientist lost his patience with the secretive Soviet representative. "This is not some little game we are playing," he shouted. "Your country is now responsible for endangering life on our planet."

Hearing of the requests, the U.S. government stepped forward to offer assistance, but the Soviets assured American scientists that they had the situation under control. At the same time that the Soviets were refusing American advice for fighting graphite fires, however, health authorities in Moscow invited Dr. Robert Gale, a widely known American surgeon, to come to the Soviet Union from his home in Los Angeles, California. This invitation alerted many Americans in the nuclear community. Gale was a world-famous specialist in bone marrow transplants—the medical procedures used in cases of severe radiation exposure.

During the first week after the explosion at Chernobyl, helicopters flew round-the-clock missions, dumping sand on the burning graphite. At the same time, Soviet officials made every effort to convey the impression that the incident was minor and "under control." In Kiev, a radio announcement several days after the accident claimed that "only two" people had been killed—suggesting that the event was little more than a small mishap. Without any proof, authorities reported that the drinking water from the reservoir near Pripyat and Kiev was safe.

The Soviet leaders wanted particularly to avoid negative publicity because of the approach of May Day, the traditional Soviet holiday on May 1. This was similar to the holiday of Labor Day in the United States, but it was particularly important in Communist nations. The entire Soviet Union celebrated with parades and patriotic ceremonies.

In Moscow, Soviet flags and decorations were displayed almost everywhere during the four-day celebration. Gorbachev appeared at the enormous May Day parade, waving at the hundreds of thousands of marchers and observers in a carefree manner. Glasnost or not, during the most important Soviet holiday of

This photograph shows one of the remote-control cleanup machines used to remove debris from the accident site. The high levels of radioactivity interfered with the machines' circuitry, causing them to malfunction. (Photo courtesy of Associated Press)

the year, any news reports of a ruined reactor and an incompetent response were forbidden. Major newspapers across the Soviet Union carried large features about the May Day celebrations. On the back pages, the news of Chernobyl was reduced to a brief note. According to the government-approved article, the radiation level had fallen "1.5 to 2 times" from the time of the accident, but the article did not state what levels had been reached at the time of the accident. Soviet television made a special note of the May Day celebrations in Kiev, with tapes of children in traditional costumes at an outdoor parade.

Outrage in Europe

The efforts to assure the Soviet people that all was returning to normal at Chernobyl did little to stem the anger across Europe. Political leaders expressed outrage with the Soviets for concealing the disaster. Sweden's energy minister, Birgitta Dahl, demanded that "the whole Soviet civilian nuclear program be subject to international control." In West Germany, Foreign Minister Hans-Dietrich Genscher insisted that Moscow shut down all nuclear power plants that used RBMK reactors. Like the Swedes, the West Germans asked that an international team be allowed to visit the site.

Health concerns were a major source of fear and anger. In Poland, which received some of its electricity from the Chernobyl plant, word of unusually high readings of radioactivity caused widespread fear. Based on the amount of radioactive particles in the air, health officials predicted a sharp increase in cancer rates for 30 years. (Statistics from the late 1990s showed an increase in some cancers, but the cause remains in dispute.) The Polish people were infuriated. A Polish citizen in Warsaw spoke for many Poles with this quote reported in *Time* magazine: "We can understand an accident. It could happen to anyone. But that the Soviets said nothing and let our children suffer exposure to this cloud for days is unforgivable."

Because the Soviets refused to issue any details about the Chernobyl event, many governments took far-reaching steps. Polish officials banned the sale of milk from cows fed on fresh grass. The government also required all children up to age 16—the age group most at risk from radiation poisoning of the thyroid gland—to take iodine tablets, a widely used protective measure against such exposure. Health officials in the United States warned women of childbearing age and all children to keep away from Poland and Scandinavia in order to avoid potential health risks. In Austria, pregnant women and children under six were advised to remain indoors until further notice. Outdoor fruit and vegetable stands across northern Europe received instructions on how to wash and cover the produce. Officials warned Swedes and Norwegians to be careful about the water they drank.

While the fear of radioactivity was reasonable, the failure of the Soviets to reveal the details of what had happened at Chernobyl created a level of anxiety approaching panic—the very reaction that Soviet officials had originally tried to avoid in Pripyat. In Oslo, Norway, callers flooded the emergency phone lines at the State Institute for Radiation Hygiene after hearing false reports of an invisible radioactive cloud over the most densely populated part of the country. A woman said, "I am a mother of small children. What measures should I take against the radiation in the air?" Another asked, "I am pregnant. Are the radiation beams dangerous to the child I am bearing?"

Despite assurances from officials that the radiation level was too low in most areas to pose a health hazard, fear spread across Europe almost as quickly as the radioactive cloud. A psychologist in Norway explained the reason for the overreaction: "We experience a danger that we cannot see and cannot register with any of our other senses, and that leads people to be worried and afraid."

The failure to directly address the Chernobyl disasters also led to false news reports that in turn led to even greater fears. As rumors grew, Kenneth Adelman, the director of the U.S. Arms

Control and Disarmament Agency, testified before Congress that the Soviet claims of only two deaths were "preposterous...in terms of an accident of this magnitude."

As alarm, fueled by rumors, spread around the word, the news media began to issue unverified reports that as many as 3,000 people had died. Great Britain and the United States advised all students and diplomatic staff living in Kiev to leave the country. On May 1, an editorial in the *New York Times* stated, "To the world outside, almost as striking as the nuclear accident that sent radioactive debris over hundreds of miles was the Soviet effort to restrict information about it." The Soviet media's response to rumors in the United States about the nuclear disaster at Chernobyl is highlighted in the "Propaganda on Soviet Television" sidebar below.

Propaganda on Soviet Television

By the time the Soviet news agency TASS announced that a disaster had occurred at Chernobyl, rumors about the number of people killed in the blast had spread to the U.S. news media. While Soviet reports claimed that two people had been killed in the blast, United Press International (UPI) reported that "eighty people died and 2,000 died on the way to the hospital." These figures made their way on to American evening news programs. These figures were never verified, but the rumor that up to 3,000 were killed in the blast persisted in the media.

Soviet officials were infuriated by what they claimed was inaccurate reporting by American news media. In response, the Soviet government's propaganda department broadcast the following statement on Soviet television on April 29.

The accident at the Chernobyl atomic power station is the first one in the Soviet Union. Similar accidents happened on several occasions in other countries. In the United States, 2,300 accidents, breakdowns, and other faults were registered in 1979 alone.... The...causes of the situation are poor quality of reactors...unsatisfactory equipment...non-observance of safety regulations and insufficient training of personnel.

As the false rumors spread, and the criticism of the Soviet system sank in, Gorbachev and his fellow Soviet leaders could no longer deny the truth. Having celebrated May Day instead of openly dealing with the disaster did little to build respect for Gorbachev internationally. The Soviets' handling of the tragedy had destroyed the world's confidence that the Soviet system had changed under its new leader. When Gorbachev received word on May 6 that the reactor fire had been smothered at last, after 10 days, he decided to address the world.

On May 14, the Soviet leader appeared on Soviet TV to give a brief speech. His remarks were broadcast around the world. Gorbachev spoke solemnly about an accident that had been described only a week before as a "minor event." This time, Gorbachev told millions around the world, "The accident at the Chernobyl nuclear plant has painfully affected the Soviet people and shocked the international community. For the first time, we confront the real force of nuclear energy out of control." (The reaction in Kiev once the disaster was confirmed is described in the "Chaos in Kiev" sidebar on this page.)

Chaos in Kiev

On May 6, Ukraine's health minister, Anatoli Romanenko, appeared on Kiev television to advise people to wash their vegetables, close their windows, and remain indoors. Within hours of Romanenko's broadcast, families began to flock to the train stations to buy tickets out of the danger zone. Traffic jams clogged the highways out of the city.

Some residents who could not leave attempted to purchase iodine tablets, an antidote for radiation poisoning. When the tablets were sold out, many residents bought iodine liquid. Drinking the liquid, which was much more powerful than tablets, sent hundreds to the hospital with serious throat damage.

Much of the radiation soon had blown northwest, away from Kiev. The amount of radiation in the city was within safe exposure limits. Yet party officials' attempts to reassure city residents were met with disbelief. The failure of the government to honestly explain the disaster at the outset pushed the city to the brink of chaos.

CHAPTER 6

The Aftermath of Chernobyl

Vendors operating fruit and vegetable stands suffered in 1998 when the government warned citizens of Kiev to avoid eating raspberries and mushrooms, both delicacies of the region, because they might have been grown in areas contaminated by the Chernobyl nuclear accident. (Photo courtesy of Associated Press)

Gorbachev's admission was an important step for him as the leader of the new Soviet policy of glasnost, but by that time, the damage from the reactor explosion could not be undone. Thirty-one people were dead or near death from the immediate effects of the blast, and hundreds in and around Chernobyl were extremely ill. Each day brought news of more misfortune that had befallen the people from Pripyat who had staffed the plant.

In northern and eastern Europe, the Chernobyl explosion mainly affected the economy, particularly the agricultural economy of the region. In Poland, Germany, Austria, and Hungary, crops were so contaminated by radiation that they had to be

destroyed. Millions of gallons of milk in Poland, Hungary, Austria, and Sweden were unusable because they came from cows that had grazed in fields contaminated with radioactive fallout. Because of the contamination, a worldwide ban on many agricultural goods produced in eastern Europe went into effect for a year. The most long-lasting effect of the radiation was on the reindeer and sheep populations in Sweden. There, the sale of milk and meat from these animals was banned in 1986 and 1987.

In all, the Chernobyl disaster caused estimated losses of more than $300 million to European agriculture, but there were no immediate health consequences for European populations. In terms of human exposure, the people of Scandinavia and eastern Europe received an amount of radiation equivalent to only one to two chest X-rays—a much smaller dose than that to which people in Chernobyl and Pripyat had been exposed.

The Sarcophagus

As alarming as the effects of Chernobyl were in areas of Europe outside the borders of the Soviet Union, the effects within the country were immeasurably worse. Even after the fires had been extinguished on May 6, radioactive particles continued to escape from the reactor core itself. Soviet engineers realized that they would need to contain this leakage to prevent further human and environmental damage.

Nuclear scientist Legasov and a panel of advisers quickly developed a plan to cover the entire reactor with a steel and concrete shell that would last "forever." The shell, nicknamed the "sarcophagus" or "coffin," would be built with 12 million cubic feet (340,000 m^3) of concrete and 3,000 tons (2,720 mt) of steel. The sarcophagus would stand 28 stories high—nearly as high as the original reactor building. Soon after the plan was announced, government energy officials insisted that the shell had to be built within months so the other reactors could be put back into service. The officials remained ignorant of the amount of cleanup and decontamination that was required before the construction could even begin.

On the grounds of the plant itself, immediate efforts were made to clear away and contain chunks of graphite and other radioactive debris. Because these objects were so *toxic,* the initial cleanup attempts were made with machines that were remote controlled. The high level of radioactivity caused their control mechanisms to malfunction, however, sending the machines crashing into each other.

After this failure, a nationwide call went out for 400,000 workers to participate in the cleanup of the plant and surrounding area. These "liquidators"—most of whom were totally unaware of the dangers of radioactivity—were allowed to be in the "hottest" areas of the power station for only 90 seconds or less at a time. Even radiation suits were insufficient protection for these workers against the amount of radioactivity in the area. Workers were given extra doses of iodine to protect their thyroid and lymph systems from radioactivity. But these procedures offered little protection against a radiation level that was 15,000 times greater than a person's normal exposure in a year. The level of radiation was so lethal that within 30 minutes on the grounds of the power station, the human nervous system would be destroyed.

Nevertheless, the promise of high pay and extra benefits not available to most Soviet citizens drew huge numbers of workers to Chernobyl. Their task was to bury the most dangerous wastes and then build the sarcophagus. Beginning in mid-May, all movable objects near the plant, including cars, trucks, and millions of cubic feet of topsoil, were buried. For several miles in every direction, trees that had absorbed the radiation were cut down and buried in concrete pits.

At this point, there were still plans to allow residents of Pripyat and Chernobyl to return to their homes. As a result, more than 60,000 buildings were washed with special decontamination chemicals, and roofs were replaced on the tallest structures, which had received the worst of the fallout. A decontamination "soap" was sprayed on streets and walkways of the two towns to prevent radioactive dust from blowing and contaminating a larger area.

The cleanup got behind schedule. Two of the reactors were restarted before the completion of the massive tomb because, according to one Soviet government official, "economic needs came uppermost" for the Communist Party leadership in Moscow. By that time, the economy of the Soviet Union was entering a stage of near-collapse. Leaving any of the nation's industrial areas without electricity would cause the collapse to occur more rapidly.

Workers and engineers ran into many problems while constructing the massive concrete and steel shell. Concrete blocks for the tomb were pieced together far from the reactor itself, but the roads entering the facilities were not wide enough to accommodate the massive loads carried by the heavy-duty construction vehicles. Once the blocks were delivered, the workers needed to put them in place. Each weighed several dozen tons, so crane operators had to perform this task. The sarcophagus would not be completed until late December 1986, two months behind schedule.

Many workers who were proud of their efforts to clean up and contain the remains of the accident at Chernobyl have since died of radiation poisoning suffered during their time as "liquidators." In this 1986 photograph, the men are holding up a sign that reads "We will fulfill the government's order." (Photo courtesy of Associated Press)

Death and Illness Descend

As hundreds of thousands of liquidators poured into the dangerous area around Chernobyl in May 1986, the first victims of extreme radiation exposure began to die. As Soviet authorities had originally claimed, the initial blast had killed only two workers at the plant, but hundreds of workers and firefighters had been exposed to massive doses of radiation.

Almost 300 people—most of them firefighters and plant workers—were hospitalized in the first 24 hours after the blast. Many had been exposed to levels of radiation 10,000 times higher than normal. Some had received such high amounts of radiation that they became radioactive themselves and poisoned the nurses and doctors caring for them. Dr. Ben, one of the first doctors to tend patients, was himself hospitalized when his hands swelled to several times their normal size from radiation poisoning. He eventually recovered.

As the health effects of the blast became clearer, Soviet doctors considered a person's distance from the blast as a way to predict the effects of the radiation. In general, anyone within 1 mile (1.6 km) of the disaster was an adult who had received lethal doses of gamma rays. These people were among the first to die, within days and weeks. Most had almost no chance of survival, and those who did survive were unlikely to live for more than five years. Anyone—men, women, or children—within a range of 3 to 4 miles (4.8 to 6.4 km), or as close as Pripyat, received beta ray exposure. At best, these people's chances of survival for more than five years were no better than 50 percent. Those who did survive longer faced potential health problems due to bone marrow destruction and intestinal damage.

The 70 workers and firefighters on the midnight shift at Chernobyl suffered beta and gamma ray exposure. Most died within 10 years. Of the hundreds of thousands of workers who participated in the cleanup, 4,000 died within 15 years. More than 70,000 were permanently disabled.

Most men, women, and children within 5 to 7 miles (8 to 11.3 km) of the accident experienced dizziness, nausea, severe diarrhea, and other symptoms of exposure to beta and alpha rays. These people were ill, but health specialists considered them unlikely to die within a five-year period—although there was no way to estimate survival beyond that time. Even smaller amounts of alpha radiation in people within 40 miles (64 km) of Chernobyl were likely to result in birth defects and increased deaths from *leukemia* and other forms of cancer by the end of the 20th century. More details on radiation exposure can be found in the "How Does Radiation Damage Health?" sidebar below.

How Does Radiation Damage Health?

Radiation can damage human health in two ways. The extent of this damage is measured by the size of the dose to which a person is exposed.

The first type of radiation damage is known as *stochastic damage,* indicating that there is a probability of illness occurring due to exposure, but its severity is uncertain. Any dose of radiation below 100 rems results in stochastic damage. This type of damage is likely to cause nausea and changes in blood cells. The probability of long-term health consequences varies by age and overall health. Thyroid cancer and leukemia can arise within two years, while other forms of cancer—such as lung, liver, and intestinal cancer—may take decades to emerge.

The second type of radiation damage, called *nonstochastic damage*, is caused by a dose of radiation exceeding 100 rems. The severity of the effect is predictable. Nonstochastic damage generally causes symptoms such as nausea, vomiting, diarrhea, and changes in blood cells. Such exposure in not immediately lethal, but there is a high probability that long-term health problems, including cancer, will occur within five years. About 50 percent of those exposed to a nonstochastic dose of radiation between 200 and 400 rems are expected to die within 30 days.

Fight to Survive

As the hospital wards filled after the explosion, it was apparent that many of those with both heat burns and radiation burns had only a minuscule chance of survival. Among the first victims, however, were those whom doctors believed could survive if they were given a bone marrow transplant. For this reason, Soviet authorities requested help from Dr. Gale, the American bone marrow transplant specialist.

Bone marrow, the soft tissue inside bones, manufactures the red blood cells that carry oxygen, cause clotting, and strengthen the immune system. Radiation has a deadly effect on marrow, and its destruction can cause death within weeks from internal bleeding and infection, but bone marrow can be replaced by marrow transplanted from a donor.

Nineteen patients from Chernobyl were taken to Moscow, where Dr. Gale performed the procedures. These patients were in danger of dying without the transplants, but they had not suffered extensive heat burns. In addition, all had parents or siblings who could supply bone marrow tissue for transplantation. As is the case with organ transplants, the tissue of the donor and the patient must match exactly. For each of the 19 operations, Gale used a syringe to draw out the donor's healthy marrow cells—usually from the hipbone—and inject them into the patient's bloodstream. In this type of procedure, the cells flow naturally to the inner areas of large bones.

By May 12, Gale had finished his work. He could only wait to see whether the victims' bodies would reject the marrow. Even if the transplants worked, Gale and the Soviet doctors knew that there was a high probability that the recipients would die of infection or other illness caused by the radiation. In fact, 11 of the 19 died within one month. None survived more than a year.

Among those for whom there was no hope of survival from marrow transplants were the firefighters who had responded to initial emergency calls. Working without masks, Lieutenant Pravik and several of his men had breathed in huge amounts of radioactivity. As the radiation progressed through their bodies, their limbs became purple and swollen. Blisters surfaced on their faces, their lips, and the insides of their mouths. Unable to eat or drink, they endured terrible suffering. More than 20 firefighters died by May 10.

Among the workers at the plant, it soon became apparent that many had only a few days at most to live. Toptunov, who had been at the controls when the accident occurred, had received devastating beta burns to his lungs. Within a week, his lung tissue rotted, and he suffocated to death on May 12. Akimov, the shift foreman, had also suffered severe beta and gamma exposure. His intestines began to disintegrate within a week. When he tried to get out of bed to go to the bathroom, he saw that the skin of one leg had turned black and slipped down to his ankle, exposing the tissue and bone. Nevertheless, he was selected for a bone marrow transplant. The last-ditch attempt failed, and he died on May 14. He was one of the 11 transplant recipients who died within a month of the blast.

Professor Guskova, in charge of evacuating people around Chernobyl, talks with Robert Gale, the American doctor who spearheaded the bone marrow transplant program for those who were severely exposed during the nuclear disaster. (Photo courtesy of CORBIS)

Benefit Concert

As news of the Chernobyl disaster spread across the Soviet Union in May 1986, young people in the country responded in a way that had become popular in the West. A benefit concert was staged on June 6. For three hours, popular Soviet rock bands with names such as Autograph, Kruiz, and Bravo played in the huge Moscow Olympic Stadium. Ticket sales raised about $150,000, which was used to provide clothing, household goods, and temporary shelter for the 92,000 people evacuated from Pripyat and other towns near the Chernobyl plant.

Unfortunately, because of the Soviet government's official disapproval of rock music and unwillingness to admit the full extent of the disaster, Soviet officials refused to allow public announcements of the concert. Moscow residents learned of the benefit only by word of mouth and from a limited number of sidewalk posters. As a result, only 25,000 attended the concert at a stadium that could hold over 100,000.

Among the other workers who were hospitalized, Yuvchenko was in some ways fortunate. He was covered with open sores on his body, and his arms would require skin grafts to replace the outer layers of skin that had been burned away, but the beta rays had not reached his internal organs or his lungs. He did recover, although he was permanently disabled.

As the spring wore on, the human toll became more disturbing. In the immediate aftermath of the explosion and fire, 299 people suffered acute radiation poisoning, and 31 died. By June, almost 150,000 people living in the worst-affected areas around Pripyat and to the north had been forced to evacuate their homes. Even those who left soon after the disaster suffered from the Soviet government's attempts to keep people uninformed about the dangers that they faced. Many of those who fled found shelter on farms or in villages that were still within range of the radioactive fallout. Yet there was no general warning about the scope of the disaster for weeks. If more inhabitants in the region had been evacuated promptly to areas far beyond the 30-mile (48-km) zone during those crucial first few days, radiation doses for many people might have been lower. Yuvchenko's young son developed thyroid cancer, as did many other children who were exposed to radiation in the hours after the blast, even though they were evacuated. (In June, money was raised for victims of the disaster, as told in the "Benefit Concert" sidebar on this page.)

A Contaminated Site

Despite the terrible toll on workers and their families, the Soviet government was more concerned with restarting the reactors than with examining the exact cause of the disaster. In November 1986, while construction of the sarcophagus was under way, Reactor Two was restarted. The restart had been delayed not only because of the ongoing cleanup, but also because a new town had to be built to house the workers who would return to run the remaining reactors.

Throughout the summer and fall of 1986, workers from every region of the Soviet Union had been brought in to build a new town 27 miles (43 km) east of Pripyat, called Slavutich. Even after apartment houses were built, however, many workers and their families were reluctant to return to the area. They were worried about radioactivity in the region and the safety of the reactors.

In 1989, when the Soviet government finally published maps of the areas affected by the disaster, it was clear that Slavutich had been built on contaminated land. The amount of radiation in the area made it unsafe to walk in the forests or to eat the mushrooms that grew there, which were a favorite delicacy of the Ukrainians. Such episodes of government misinformation deepened the Ukrainian citizens' mistrust of their Communist leaders.

Distributing Blame

Both Dyatlov and Brukhanov had been exposed to high doses of radiation, but doctors predicted that they would survive at least five years. The main problems that they faced in the aftermath of the disaster were legal rather than medical. In early 1987, Brukhanov, Dyatlov, and four other managers of the Chernobyl plant were put on trial for their roles in the disaster. Dyatlov had turned off the plant's emergency system. Brukhanov had been away from the plant during the crucial test. The Soviet government

Russian prime minister Mikhail Kasyanov, left, and Ukrainian president Leonid Kuchma, right, stand in silence at a memorial event at the Chernobyl nuclear power plant in December 2000. The power plant was decommissioned and shut down the following day. (Photo courtesy of Associated Press)

claimed that they had been incompetent in running the plant and that they had mishandled the emergency afterward. The authorities overlooked the fact that high-level Communist energy ministers had pressured these men. The government also refused to examine the actual flaws of the RBMK reactor itself, because to do so might mean that all Soviet nuclear plants would have to be shut down.

The trials of Brukhanov and the other managers were covered publicly, because Soviet leaders wanted to emphasize that the Chernobyl disaster had been caused by incompetent management and not by flawed reactors. To that end, for example, the Soviet-controlled newspaper *Pravda* reported that "the accident occurred because of a series of...violations of rules of operation by the [managers] of the power station." All were found guilty of criminal negligence. Brukhanov and Dyatlov were sentenced to 10 years in prison.

Soon after they entered prison, a scientific commission that included Legasov issued a report on the causes of the disaster. Part of the blame fell on the RBMK reactor itself. A thorough study showed that these reactors were unstable at low power, which could lead to a rapid, uncontrollable power increase. This excess power caused water in the cooling and circulation pipes to heat too rapidly. This, in turn, led to an increase of steam pressure, similar to an overheated radiator in a car. The process eventually built up to what was termed a "burn-up" of the core, rather than the more commonly known problem, a meltdown.

The investigative commission also mentioned human error as a contributing factor in the disaster. During the turbine test, only 11 control rods had been in the reactor core, despite a standard order that a minimum of 30 rods—of a total of 211—should be in the core at all times. In addition, the reactor's emergency alert system had been disabled.

Although Dyatlov and Brukhanov were already serving prison sentences by this time, Legasov's commission declared that blaming only human failure was as unproductive as blaming an accidental shooting on "those who hang the rifle on the wall aware that it is loaded, or those who inadvertently pull the trigger." The commission recommended that additional control rods be added to each reactor. The new rods, the commissioners wrote, should be able to be scrammed within 4 seconds rather than the much slower 18 to 20 seconds required at the Chernobyl plant. They also recommended that update manuals and training be provided to operators at the power plants.

CHAPTER 7

The Legacy of Chernobyl

As events played out, neither Brukhanov nor Dyatlov served their full 10 years. Both were released in 1992. Both men died of cancer shortly after their release from prison.

During this time, momentous changes had occurred. In August 1991, the Soviet Union ceased to exist as a sovereign nation. In the final years of the Soviet Union, Soviet power and prestige had been weakened by popular political movements in eastern Europe—particularly in Poland, Romania, East Germany, and Czechoslovakia—that led to the beginnings of democratic systems in those states and the reunification of East Germany with West Germany. Soviet political leaders failed to recognize that the system was breaking down and required massive change.

Hans Blix, chairman of the Chernobyl Shelter Project's Assembly of Donors, is part of a delegation that monitors the progress of work reinforcing the deteriorating sarcophagus over the exploded reactor. In this 2003 photograph, Blix passes through a radiation checkpoint within the plant. (Photo courtesy of Associated Press)

Many old-style Soviet military leaders refused to accept any change. Their unsuccessful attempt to depose Gorbachev, foiled by the leader of the Russian Federation, Boris Yeltsin, signaled the end of the Soviet Union.

In the uncertain period of the late 1980s, Legasov had been prominent among the high-ranking officials who attempted to persuade the conservative political leadership to change its style of rule. But the Soviet political establishment ignored his recommendations for changes in the operation and training at nuclear power plants. Unable to overcome depression that was caused by the terrible aftermath of Chernobyl, Legasov committed suicide in 1989.

By late 1991, the Soviet Union had broken up into 15 independent nations. One of those nations was the Republic of Ukraine. One of the first and most lasting issues that the new government faced was Chernobyl. Like a ripple from a stone thrown into a pond, the health effects of the disaster had spread since 1986.

By April 1992, according to Ukraine's minister for Chernobyl, Georgii Gotovchits, between 6,000 and 8,000 people had died in Ukraine as a result of the Chernobyl disaster. Many of them had lived in the contaminated areas and had suffered radiation-related health problems, such as cardiovascular disease and intestinal cancers.

Because of the often uncertain link between radiation exposure and eventual health problems, solid statistics were often difficult to determine. The former Soviet province of Belarus, now an independent nation, had been directly in the path of the radiation from Chernobyl. In 1992 it was reported that more than 2 million people, including more than 660,000 children, lived in contaminated zones in Belarus. People who live in these areas are assumed to have consumed contaminated food and inhaled radioactive particles shortly after the accident.

The effects of the disaster on people were found to vary according to their distance from the disaster and length of exposure. One study was commissioned in 1992 by Ukraine's government. This study claimed that of the 400,000 liquidators involved in cleanup operations, about 25,000 had died. A Soviet study completed in 1990 before the collapse of the government put the number of liquidator deaths at about 8,500. Final numbers were difficult to assess, because in the years immediately after the disaster, the medical records of soldiers who had worked as liquidators were classified as top secret. Those who had survived suffered from conditions typical of radiation poisoning, such as lung cancer, leukemia, heart disease, and intestinal disorders.

One official who studied the effects of Chernobyl stated the following in 1992:

> We...[do] not know the precise number of deaths, though from my own experience I know many...who died...mostly from heart attacks. These men were in their late twenties or thirties....A recent figure...declared that 5,000 people had...died...and...more than 500,000 people were exposed to radiation, so [a 10 percent death rate for those exposed] is a plausible percentage.

Each year throughout the 1990s, reports of the effects of Chernobyl continued to offer grim information. By 1993, Ukraine's health ministry had compiled a registry of 576,000 people in that country alone who were at risk of developing cancer or other diseases as a result of radiation exposure. Many officials estimated that at least 4 million people will be affected—most in the western area of the former Soviet Union. Radiation levels remained extremely high in parts of Belarus, Ukraine, and Russia.

Despite the enormous damage done to the people of Ukraine and surrounding areas, the Chernobyl nuclear plant continued to operate with three RBMK reactors. The plant operators, however, did institute the recommended changes in the number of control rods kept in the core. In 1993 a fire in Reactor Two forced it to shut down. Reactor One was shut down in 1996. Finally, in 2000, the Chernobyl plant closed permanently.

Not long after the shutdown, a radiation leak was detected from the sarcophagus covering Reactor Four. Since 2001, the government of Ukraine has sought international funds to help rebuild the outer protective shell.

Land Laid Waste

Scientists believe that the damage from the Chernobyl disaster will never truly come to an end. In addition to the human lives that were destroyed, a way of life for millions was ruined. Agricultural effects of the disaster, for example, will continue many years after the more immediate health effects cease.

Mutations of various lines of livestock, as well as food crops, have appeared since 1986. A newspaper reporter described a visit to a farm north of Pripyat in 1992: "At the farm…I was shown a suckling pig whose head looked like that of a frog; instead of eyes there were large tissue outgrowths with no cornea or pupil. 'They usually die soon after birth but this one has survived,' the owner explained."

In 1996, 10 years after the disaster, the total area of land in Ukraine still registering higher than normal radiation readings

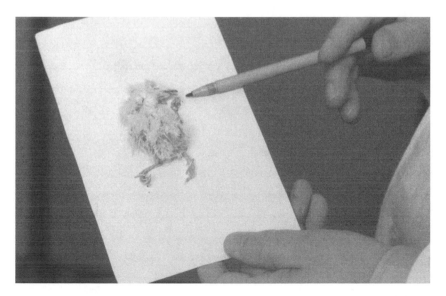

Since the nuclear explosion at Chernobyl in 1986, hundreds of cases of deformed livestock, as far as 120 miles (193 km) from the disaster site, have been reported. This photograph shows a stuffed chicken born with four wings. (Photo courtesy of Associated Press)

was over 13,500 square miles (35,000 km^2)—more than 5 percent of the nation's total area. The most heavily contaminated parts of Ukraine contained 1,300 towns and villages with a total population of 2.6 million, including 700,000 children. The land within an 18.6-mile (30-km) circle of the Chernobyl plant was largely uninhabited. Formerly busy communities were ghost towns. A barbed wire fence encircled the once-modern town of Pripyat to prevent former residents from returning to claim belongings that they left behind.

Among the most famous athletes of the former Soviet Union is Olympic gymnast Olga Korbut, who grew up about 180 miles (290 km) from Chernobyl. Much of her once-beautiful native land has been heavily contaminated with radiation from Chernobyl. Plant and animal species have died out. Soil and water are poisoned. In an interview in 1998, she described how children in her hometown are now taught about nature—by observing special indoor exhibits. "In an area long known for its wild mushrooms, berries, flowers and the beauty of its forests," said Korbut, "the children are no longer allowed to go into the woods."

The Human Toll

In 2002 a UN study of the region most directly harmed by the disaster found that the people faced enormous health, economic, and psychological problems. The three hardest-hit countries—Belarus, Russia, and Ukraine—became independent nations after the collapse of the Soviet Union. These countries, with a total population of more than 5.5 million people, have struggled to provide care for the victims of Chernobyl while also attempting to become economically healthy democracies. Health care costs alone in the three countries totaled billions of dollars by the early 21st century.

The Ukrainian government agency Chernobyl Interinform reported in March 2002 that 84 percent of the 3 million people in

Ukraine who had been exposed to radiation from Chernobyl had fielded claims to receive extra health benefits. Not all were for radioactivity-related cancer. "After the Chernobyl disaster, a massive increase in non-malignant diseases was also observed in the population," wrote Dr. Edmund Lengfelder, a German specialist in radiation medicine, 15 years after the accident.

An increased incidence of breast cancer as a direct consequence of the accident was noted in 2002 by a team of international specialists. The number of cases has doubled in Belarus. Health specialists from Belarus and Ukraine also predict an increase in intestinal tumors and higher-than-normal incidence of lung and stomach cancer among the male population of the severely contaminated areas.

In addition, there is general agreement that more than 2,000 children and adolescents in the most severely contaminated areas of Belarus contracted cancer of the thyroid because of the reactor disaster. This coincides with statistics from Ukraine's ministry for Chernobyl that show an extraordinary rise in thyroid cancer among children living in the contaminated zone. Before the Chernobyl accident in 1986, for example, only two cases of thyroid tumors among children were diagnosed in all of Ukraine. But in 1990, the total among children living in the contaminated zone was 29. In April 1993, more than 200 such cases were reported among children living in northwest Ukraine. In all, the number of thyroid cancer cases among those who were children and adolescents at the time of the accident may reach 8,000 by 2010.

Even that figure, however, is considered low. Specialists for the World Health Organization (WHO) predict that as many as 50,000 people who were children in 1986 will develop thyroid cancer. Lengfelder, who has run a thyroid cancer center in Belarus since 1991, believes that more than 100,000 additional cases of thyroid cancer in all age groups will arise by 2010. UN secretary general Kofi Annan stated, "At least three million children in Belarus, Ukraine and the Russian Federation require physical treatment due to the Chernobyl accident. Not until 2016, at the earliest, will we know the full number of those likely to develop serious medical conditions." One psychological disorder that resulted from the disaster is highlighted in "The Chernobyl Syndrome" sidebar on page 79.

Nuclear Power after Chernobyl

Because it so closely followed the Three Mile Island event in 1979, the Chernobyl disaster created an awareness of nuclear power safety in the international community that was much greater than before. But despite widespread concerns about the risks of nuclear power, officials were quick to point out that those two events were the only major nuclear accidents to have occurred in years of operation at plants in 32 countries.

Nevertheless, international organizations, such as the IAEA and the Organization for Economic Cooperation and Development (OECD), as well as agencies in countries with nuclear power plants, such as the U.S. Nuclear Regulatory Commission (NRC), reexamined power plants and procedures around the world after Chernobyl. Investigations led to a new focus on the human factors of nuclear safety. No major design changes were called for in Western reactors, but controls were improved and operator training was updated.

The first efforts to examine the safety of reactors themselves focused on plants in the former Soviet Union—primarily Russia and Lithuania. Beginning in 1992, a major international program of assistance by the OECD, IAEA, and Commission of European Communities attempted to bring the Soviet-designed RBMK reactors up to Western safety standards and improve plant operations. Modifications were made to RBMK reactors in Russia and Lithuania that addressed the cause of the Chernobyl blast. Automated inspection equipment was also installed in these reactors to avoid the possibility of human error.

The IAEA gave high priority to the safety of nuclear power plants in eastern Europe, where deficiencies similar to those in the old Soviet plants remained. Unfortunately, demand for energy in these countries (Poland, Romania, and others) did not permit them to close any plants for evaluation. The concern for plant safety led the European Union (EU)—an organization of European nations—to require plant shutdowns and inspections in any countries seeking EU membership.

Throughout the 1990s, there was an increased amount of international cooperation on nuclear safety issues. In 1990 the International Nuclear Event Scale (INES) was developed by the IAEA and OECD to communicate and evaluate reported nuclear incidents to the public. The scale runs from zero, meaning an event with no safety significance, to 7, for a "major accident" such as Chernobyl. The Three Mile Island event rated a 5 for an "accident with off-site risk." A level 4 incident was an "accident without significant off-site risk." The incident that occurred in Japan in September 1999 was considered a level 4.

In 1996 the Nuclear Safety Convention, a meeting of nations that generate nuclear power, formed the first international legal commission with the power to assess the safety of nuclear power plants worldwide. Sixty-five participating countries agreed to maintain a high level of safety by meeting agreed-upon international standards and reporting any failure to meet those standards to the commission.

The Chernobyl Syndrome

The events of April 1986 and the ensuing years have created what specialists call the Chernobyl Syndrome. This psychological condition of extreme stress among people in Belarus, Russia, and Ukraine is characterized by people's overwhelming uncertainty about the effects of the disaster on the health of themselves and their children. This feeling of helplessness has led to increased alcoholism and clinical depression in millions. A 2002 UN report titled *The Human Consequences of the Chernobyl Nuclear Accident* suggests that people feel they are victims of events over which they have no influence. They have little confidence in their own ability to improve their situation.

CHAPTER 8

Conclusion

The Chernobyl zone is one of the most dangerously radioactive places in the world today. Tons of nuclear fuel still remain underneath the concrete sarcophagus over Reactor Four. The radiation level in the reactor itself is fatal to any life, and the nuclear night-

A pine sapling about 1 mile (1.6 km) from the Chernobyl plant bears sickly brown branches in this photo taken in late 2000. The sickly branches are mutations caused by radiation exposure as a result of the 1986 explosion. (Photo courtesy of Associated Press)

mare continues to spread. In the 18.6-mile (30-km) zone around the reactor are more than 800 clay-lined burial pits. These were constructed in 1986 by the liquidators to cover radioactive waste, including trees that absorbed radioactivity from the atmosphere. Recently, it was discovered that many of these dumps have leaked. The poison seeping from them has contaminated the bottom soil in the Dnieper River and its tributary, the Pripyat. Sediment taken from these rivers has been found to contain strontium, cesium, and plutonium. These two rivers supply water for 30 million people. In order to prevent further contamination of water sources, the wastes must be removed to properly designed waste storage facilities—yet these facilities have not yet been built.

Not surprisingly, disaster-related health expenses have had a damaging effect on the economies of Ukraine, Russia, and Belarus. The people living in contaminated areas have struggled more than other citizens to make new lives for themselves in depressed economies. But few have been able to leave the affected villages and towns where their families have lived for generations because they are extremely poor and have no means of further support.

At the turn of the century, UN agencies became more actively involved in addressing the long-term problems caused by the Chernobyl disaster. The WHO and the Food and Agriculture Organization (FAO) were among several agencies that created community assistance and economic development projects. The IAEA also established the International Chernobyl Research Network to continue study of the long-term effects of radiation. Among the nations that have contributed the most financially to this organization is Japan. Japanese government and private donations to Chernobyl research reached $100 million by 2002. Japanese experts who studied the long-term effects of the bombing of Hiroshima and Nagasaki assisted in much of the early work of the new UN Chernobyl efforts.

At the end of 2001, there were 435 nuclear power plants known to be in operation worldwide. These plants generated about 17 percent of the electricity used around the world. The construction of new nuclear plants, however, has come to a virtual halt in most nations since 1998. One exception is China, which had six nuclear power plants in 2003 and planned to have 50 plants in operation by 2020.

Would news of a Chernobyl-like accident in any operating nuclear plant spread more quickly today than it did in 1986? The answer to this question might depend on the location of the plant itself. In politically open countries such as France or Japan that draw more than half their electricity from nuclear power, news of even the slightest nuclear accident would be announced immediately. On the other hand, in closed societies such as North Korea, China, or Iran, such an event might be treated differently. News travels much faster today over cable television and the Internet than it did in the 1980s. Satellites and computer systems might alert the public to such a disaster more rapidly. But the determination of whether modern technology could prevent the repercussions of rumors and propaganda is only theoretical.

Human history from the beginning of time has been affected by disasters that killed millions and destroyed enormous areas. But the disaster at Chernobyl was greater than a fire, an earthquake, or a flood. Chernobyl was a disaster that affected the entire planet. In a way, it was the first great disaster created by modern technology.

Shortly after he was arrested and prepared to stand trial, Anatoli Dyatlov wrote a letter to a friend describing his reaction on April 26, 1986, a few moments after 1:23 A.M. (EEST), when his life—and the lives of millions of other people—changed forever. "It seemed as if the world was coming to an end.... I could not believe my eyes; I saw the reactor ruined by the explosion. I was the first man in the world to see this. As a nuclear engineer, I realized all the consequences of what had happened. It was a nuclear hell."

Time Line

1986

April 25, 1:00 a.m. (EEST)	Reactor Four at the Chernobyl power plant is running at full power with normal operation; slowly, operators reduce power for a test
April 25, 1:05 p.m. (EEST)	Twelve hours after power reduction is initiated, the reactor reaches 50 percent power; Turbine Seven is switched off
April 25, 2:00 p.m. (EEST)	According to the plan for the test, the reactor's power is to be reduced to 30 percent. Energy authorities in Kiev suddenly refuse to allow this because of an unforeseen electricity demand. Reactor Four remains at 50 percent power for the next nine hours.
April 26, 12:28 a.m. (EEST)	The Chernobyl staff receives permission to resume the power reduction; power in Reactor Four falls below 7 percent
April 26, 1:00–1:20 a.m. (EEST)	The operators force the reactor up to 7 percent power by removing all but 11 of the control rods; the reactor becomes increasingly unstable
April 26, 1:22 a.m. (EEST)	Operators, believing that they have stable conditions, decide to start the test
April 26, 1:23 a.m. (EEST)	The test begins, once the remaining turbine is shut down
April 26, 1:23:40 a.m. (EEST)	Power in the reactor begins to rise rapidly

Photo courtesy of Associated Press

April 26, 1:23:44 a.m. (EEST)	The reactor reaches 100 times full power; the radioactive fuel disintegrates, and excess steam, which was supposed to go to the turbines, breaks containment tubes; explosions blow off the top shield of the reactor
April 27, 2:00 p.m. (EEST)	The evacuation of Pripyat begins
April 28	Soviet television announces the accident to the world
April 29	The first news item about the disaster is published in the Soviet newspaper *Pravda*
May 2	A 20-mile (32-km) zone around the plant is designated for evacuation
May 10	The fourth reactor is capped with sand and boron, and leakages of radiation end
May 14	Soviet premier Mikhail Gorbachev admits the serious accident at Chernobyl to the world in a televised speech
May–June	Military reservists are brought to Chernobyl to lead the cleanup operation
November	The new workers' village of Slavutich is completed; the remaining power plant reactors are restarted
December	The concrete sarcophagus over the fourth reactor is completed

1987

July

Chernobyl director Victor Brukhanov and five plant operators, including Anatoli Dyatlov, are found guilty of gross negligence at a trial held mostly on camera in the town of Chernobyl

1989

February

The first maps highlighting radiation fallout from Chernobyl are published in the Soviet press

Photo courtesy of Associated Press

Chronology of Nuclear Plant Accidents

The following list is a selection of major nuclear plant accidents of the last 60 years.

1952

December 12

Chalk River, Ontario, Canada

Partial reactor core meltdown; none killed

1955

November 10

Idaho Falls, Idaho, United States

Partial reactor core meltdown; none killed

1957

September 29

Chelyabinsk, Soviet Union

Nuclear waste storage tank explosion; none killed

October 10

Near Liverpool, England

Uranium fire; none killed

1958

October 18

Vinca, Yugoslavia

Overheated reactor; 1 killed

December 30

Los Alamos, New Mexico, United States

Plutonium exposure; 1 killed

1961

January 3

Idaho Falls, Idaho, United States

Explosion; 3 killed

1966

October 5

Lagoona Beach, Michigan, United States

Partial reactor core meltdown; none killed

Photo courtesy of Associated Press

1969

January 21

Lucens, Switzerland

Radiation leak; none killed

1971

November 19

Monticello, Minnesota, United
States

Nuclear waste water storage
facility overflow; none killed

1975

March 22

Decatur, Alabama, United
States

Reactor fire; none killed

November 30

Leningrad, Soviet Union

Fuel assembly rupture; none
killed

1979

March 28

Near Harrisburg, Pennsylvania,
United States

Partial reactor core meltdown;
none killed

1981

February 11

Sequoyah, Tennessee, United
States

Coolant leak; none killed

March 8

Tsuruga, Japan

Nuclear waste water leak; none
killed

1982

January 25

Near Rochester, New York,
United States

Steam pipe rupture; none killed

1985

June 27

Balakovo, Soviet Union

Steam leak; 14 killed

1986

April 26

Chernobyl, Ukraine, Soviet
Union

Reactor explosion and fire; 31
killed

January 4

Gore, Oklahoma, United States

Chemical storage tank
explosion; 1 killed

1989

November 24

Greifswald, Germany

Partial reactor core meltdown; none killed

1997

May 14

Near Richland, Washington, United States

Chemical storage tank explosion; none killed

1999

September 30

Tokaimura, Japan

Uranium exposure; 1 killed

2003

April 10

Paks, Hungary

Gas leak; none killed

Photo courtesy of Associated Press

Glossary

alpha rays   The least deadly radioactive rays

atom   The smallest part of an element that can exist alone or in combination

beta rays   The second-most deadly radioactive rays

chain reaction   A self-sustaining chemical or nuclear effect yielding energy or products that cause additional and similar reactions

Communist   Referring to a system of government in which there is no private property

control rods   Devices used to control the chain reaction in nuclear reactors; made of the element boron

core   The central part of a nuclear reactor, where atomic fission occurs

element   A substance that cannot be chemically broken down

fallout   Microscopic particles of debris in the atmosphere following an explosion, especially radioactive debris after a nuclear explosion

fission   A process by which an atomic nucleus (usually of uranium) is split into fragments (usually two fragments of comparable mass), releasing large quantities of energy

gamma rays   The most deadly radioactive rays

glasnost   Russian for "openness"; the name of a government policy of the Soviet Union in the 1980s

leukemia   Cancer of the bone marrow that results in uncontrolled production of white blood cells, leading to iron deficiency, impaired blood clotting, and enlargement of the lymph nodes, liver, and spleen

mutation   A sudden change in cell structure that is passed on to daughter cells; may be caused by exposure to radiation

neutron   A subatomic particle in the nucleus of an atom that binds protons together

nuclear   Describes a form of energy arising from particles found in atomic nuclei

nuclear reactor   A piece of equipment within which a chain reaction is initiated and controlled; the resulting heat is typically used for power generation or military, experimental, or medical purposes

nucleus   The center of an atom, made up of protons and neutrons

periodic table   A table that groups the elements by atomic number, resulting in a pattern in which similar properties recur periodically by element

plutonium   A naturally radioactive element occurring in uranium ores that is a by-product of fission and is used in nuclear weapons; it is absorbed by bone marrow and is very toxic to plants and animals, including humans

proton   A subatomic particle in an atom's nucleus that carries a positive charge

rad   "Radiation absorbed dose"; a measure of radiation hitting the human body

radioactivity   The emission of radiation from unstable atomic nuclei or as a consequence of a nuclear reaction

rem   "Roentgen equivalent, man"; a measure of the effects of different types of radioactive rays on humans

roentgen   The original unit used to measure radiation exposure

toxic   Highly poisonous

turbine   A cylindrical machine in which energy is converted to mechanical or electrical power

unstable   A term used to describe elements with large numbers of protons and neutrons in the nucleus; an unstable atom is easier to split than a stable atom

uranium   A silvery-white, metallic element that is radioactive and toxic to plants and animals, including humans; extracted from the minerals uraninite and carnotite, it is used in research, nuclear fuels, and nuclear weapons

Further Reading and Web Sites

Brennan, Kristine. *The Chernobyl Nuclear Disaster.* Broomall, Pa.: Chelsea House, 2001. A book about the Chernobyl disaster for readers in grades five to eight.

Bryan, Nichol. *Chernobyl: Nuclear Disaster.* Milwaukee: World Almanac, 2003. This book describes the environmental effects of the Chernobyl disaster and the lessons learned about the future of energy.

California National Guard: International Affairs—Chernobyl Timeline. A calendar of events from initial construction of the Chernobyl plant until final closure in 2000. Available online. URL: http://www.calguard.ca.gov/ia/Chernobyl-timeline.htm. Accessed September 3, 2004.

Chernobyl Children's Project (UK). This British charity web site has links to a history of the disaster, its long-term effects, the latest information, and ways to donate money. Available online. URL: http://www.chernobyl-children.org.uk/. Accessed September 3, 2004.

Chernobyl.com—Chernobyl Information. The International Chernobyl Research and Information Network has extensive links to history, studies, and interviews. Available online. URL: http://www.chernobyl.com/info.htm. Accessed September 3, 2004.

Chernobyl Nuclear Disaster. A well-organized web site about the event, its immediate aftermath, and the long-term environmental damage. Available online. URL: http://www.chernobyl.co.uk/. Accessed September 3, 2004.

CNN.com—Chernobyl: An Unthinkable Disaster. A time line of the event as it unfolded, as well as world reaction as the news was announced. Available online. URL: http://www.cnn.com/

2000/WORLD/europe/06/05/ukraine.chernobyl/index.html. Accessed September 3, 2004.

Cole, Michael D. *Three Mile Island: Nuclear Disaster.* Berkeley Heights, N.J.: Enslow Publishers, Inc., 2002. A detailed version of the Three Mile Island accident, with background on nuclear power, glossary, chapter notes, and bibliography.

Condon, Judith. *Chernobyl and Other Nuclear Accidents.* Austin, Tex.: Raintree Steck-Vaughn, 1998. A book about the Chernobyl and Three Mile Island disasters, as well as nuclear weapons accidents.

Dowswell, Paul. *The Chernobyl Disaster.* Austin, Tex.: Raintree Steck-Vaughn, 2004. An informative, up-to-date book about the disaster.

Fusco, Paul, and Magdalena Caris. *Chernobyl Legacy.* Cincinnati, Ohio: F&W Publications, 2001. Photographs and texts 15 years after the disaster document people affected by Chernobyl.

HowStuffWorks—How Nuclear Power Works. An easy-to-understand explanation of nuclear energy. Available online. URL: http://science.howstuffworks.com/nuclear-power1.htm. Accessed September 3, 2004.

International Atomic Energy Agency (IAEA)—Chernobyl Plus 15. A site with frequently asked questions about Chernobyl. Available online. URL: http://www.iaea.org/NewsCenter/Features/Chernobyl-15/cherno-faq.shtml. Accessed September 3, 2004.

International Chernobyl Research and Information Network (ICRIN)—Chernobyl.info: The Chernobyl Accident— The Explosion of the Reactor. Gives a detailed explanation of the Chernobyl explosion. Available online. URL: http://www.chernobyl.info/en/Facts/Accident/Explosion. Accessed September 3, 2004.

Mayel, Mark. *Nuclear Accidents.* San Diego: Lucent Books, 2003. A book about nuclear power accidents and weapons mishaps, including the sinking of nuclear-powered submarines.

McQuery, Maureen. *Nuclear Legacy: Students of Two Atomic Cities.* Columbus, Ohio: Batelle Press, 2000. A book of interviews with teenagers in Slavutich, Ukraine, near the Chernobyl plant, and in the Tri-Cities area of Washington State, near the Hanford nuclear research facility, which produced the plutonium for the first atomic bomb.

Medvedev, Grigori. *The Truth about Chernobyl.* New York: Basic Books, 1992. An engineer at Chernobyl during its original construction describes the events leading up to and following the blast.

Medvedev, Zhores. *The Legacy of Chernobyl.* New York: W.W. Norton, 1992. A Soviet physicist describes the events of the disaster and argues that reactor design rather than human error was to blame.

Mould, R.F. *Chernobyl Record: The Definitive History of the Chernobyl Catastrophe.* Philadelphia: Institute of Physics Publishing, 2000. A scientific record of the events leading up to the blast and the aftermath, with eyewitness interviews.

Nuclear Energy Agency (NEA)—Chernobyl: Assessment of Radiological and Health Impacts. An article on the Chernobyl disaster and its impact after 15 years. Available online. URL: http://www.nea.fr/html/rp/chernobyl/chernobyl.html. Accessed September 3, 2004.

Nuclearfiles.org—Nuclear Accidents Time Line. A listing of significant nuclear accidents worldwide since the beginning of the nuclear age. Available online. URL: http://www.nuclearfiles.org/hitimeline/nwa/. Accessed November 12, 2004.

O'Meara, Liam. *Fallout: Children of Belarus and the People of Ireland after Chernobyl.* Dublin, Ireland: Columba Press, 2003. People from Ireland aid in the care of children in Belarus who were born handicapped as a result of the radiation from the Chernobyl accident.

Oracle ThinkQuest Education Foundation—Chernobyl: A Nuclear Disaster. A very informative site developed by U.S. high school students for national science competition. Available online. URL: http://library.thinkquest.org/3426/index.html. Accessed September 3, 2004.

Petryna, Adriana. *Life Exposed: Biological Citizens after Chernobyl.* Princeton, N.J.: Princeton University Press, 2002. Observations and interviews with people in Ukraine and Belarus affected by the Chernobyl disaster.

Read, Piers Paul. *Ablaze: The Story of the Victims and Heroes of Chernobyl.* New York: Random House, 1993. The definitive and most complete account of the event for readers at a high school level and above.

solcomhouse—Nuclear Power. This site gives a clear explanation of nuclear reactors, as well as a link to a detailed article on the Three Mile Island accident. Available online. URL: http://www.solcomhouse.com/nuclear.htm. Accessed September 3, 2004.

The United Nations (UN) and Chernobyl. A history of the disaster and UN efforts in the region for the past 18 years. Available online. URL: http://www.un.org/ha/chernobyl/. Accessed September 3, 2004.

World Nuclear Association (WNA)—Information and Issue Briefs. A list of short WNA publications that are updated regularly. The briefs cover every aspect of nuclear power. Available online. URL: http://www.world-nuclear.org/info/info.htm. Accessed November 12, 2004.

Index